THE

"PARISH TRACTS,"

BEING A

SERIES OF PLAIN TRACTS

FOR

DISTRIBUTION IN EITHER TOWN OR COUNTRY PARISHES.

BY

J. HARRY BUCHANAN, M.A.

SOLD ONLY BY THE AUTHOR,
ILKESTON, NOTTS.

Price 1s. 6d.

THE

"PARISH TRACTS,"

BEING A

SERIES OF PLAIN TRACTS

FOR

DISTRIBUTION IN EITHER TOWN OR COUNTRY PARISHES.

BY

J. HARRY BUCHANAN, M.A.

SOLD ONLY BY THE AUTHOR,
ILKESTON, NOTTS.

Price 1s. 6d.

CONTENTS.

—: o :—

PREFACE.

—:o:—

SINCE its inauguration, fifty years ago, a conspicuous part in the great Church revival of our day has been played by Tracts. The "Tracts for the Times," with which the movement may be said to have started, were but the forerunners of innumerable little theological *brochures*, with which the catalogues of our Church booksellers still teem. Addressed, for the most part, *ad clerum*, the influence of the "Tracts for the Times" on the middle and lower classes was but an indirect influence. Nor was it otherwise with, perhaps, the majority of the later productions referred to. Valuable as many of these unquestionably were, the direct impression left by their perusal on the imperfectly educated mind, was not great. Often their style was too diffuse, or their phraseology too scientific, or their theology wanting in accuracy. Too much knowledge on the part of those to whom they were addressed, was assumed. No wonder that they not unfrequently missed the mark. In the present series, these defects, as it seems to me, are avoided. At any rate, it must be admitted that these Tracts do not err on the side of prolixity. They are not, nor are intended to be, exhaustive. Their value consists in their theological accuracy, their brevity, and the intelligibleness of their language. Issuing at intervals from the same quiver, they were designed to serve the purpose of darts (*Jacula Prudentum*, as George Herbert would say), each with a special aim, and that aim to draw attention, in plain unmistakable words, to some one truth, or aspect of the Truth, or duty arising out of the Truth. The Tracts have already been found eminently useful, both in this country and in the Colonies. May God's blessing abide on this and all other efforts to glorify Him by edifying His Church.

H. L. JENNER,

Bishop.

PRESTON VICARAGE,

February 10th, 1882.

ADVERTISEMENT.

—: 0 :—

I ISSUE this volume of my Tracts, bound, in answer to a kind but distinct call on the part of the public. Some of the Tracts, in the course of revisal, have been slightly, but not materially, altered. All the Tracts may still be had in their loose form for distribution at 3s. per 100 post free. I wish to express my gratitude to the Right Rev. Bishop Jenner for so kindly undertaking to furnish my little volume with a preface, and I am scarcely less indebted to those learned Divines and Theologians who have, with equal kindness, revised those of my Tracts which, from their dogmatic character, required very careful wording.

J. HARRY BUCHANAN.

ILKESTON,

Quinquagesima. 1882.

The Parish Tracts.

No. I.

"THE REASON WHY."

In these days everyone wants a reason for every-thing. That is quite right. To do anything unless you know "*the reason why*" you did it, is to act like a child or a madman; for both of these act according to impulse, and not according to reason. Let me then give you the "reasons why" you should fulfil the following religious duties :—

1.—You should attend Church worship and no other, BECAUSE the Church is "the Body of Christ," (Col. i. 24); "The pillar and ground of the Truth," (1 Tim. ii. 15); because "Christ loved the Church and gave Himself for it," (Eph. v. 25); and because Holy Scripture, in these and many other like passages has reference *only* to the Holy Catholic and Apostolic Church, founded by Christ and His Apotles, and which alone has Divine Authority to " disciple all nations," to preach the Gospel, and administer the Holy Sacraments. If a

B

man "neglect to hear the Church, let him be unto thee as an heathen man." (S. Matt. xviii. 17.)

2.—You should be a Communicant, BECAUSE in the Blessed Sacrament Christ offers you, "verily and indeed," His Body and Blood to be a means of *Life* to your soul, and "Except ye eat the Flesh of the Son of Man, and drink His Blood, ye have no life in you. (S. John vi. 53).

3.—You should, if health permit, always receive the Holy Sacrament at an early Service rather than at a late one, BECAUSE such sacred Food ought certainly to be the first food which passes your lips, and by going to an early Service you can wait for your breakfast till you go home.

4.—You should not stay away from the Holy Table on the excuse of "*not being fit*," BECAUSE if you are "not fit" for that, you are certainly "not fit" to die, and it is your duty to make yourself fit. If you have any special difficulties ask advice and ghostly counsel of your Parish Clergyman, who is "set over you in the Lord," and who will be always glad to help you.

5.—If you desire to die in the Lord you must live in Him; and this you cannot do unless you are in daily communion with Him. You should therefore never omit to say *private prayers every*

morning on rising, and every night on going to
bed; BECAUSE, Scripture instructs you thus:
" When thou prayest, enter into thy closet,
and when thou hast shut thy door, pray to thy
Father which is in secret, and thy Father
which seeth in secret shall reward thee openly.
(S. Matt. vi. 6.)

6.—Whenever there is an offering of Alms in
   Church you should give something, little or
   much, in accordance with your power; BECAUSE,
   whatever you give in Church you give to God,
   and it is surely right that you should give back
   something to Him, seeing that He gives all to
   you :—" Every good gift * * * cometh
   down from the Father, (S. James i. 17); and
   the offering of Alms on Sunday is a strictly
   Apostolic command :—" Upon the *first day of
   the week* let every one of you lay by him in
   store, as God hath prospered him." (1 Cor.
   xvi. 2).

7.—Lastly, and more important, if possible, than
   all :—Try and live in Charity with all your
   neighbours, " If it be possible * * * live
   peacably with all men." (Rom. xii. 18). Do
   not say unkind things of them, even if true, for
   you are not their judge; " Who art thou that
   judgest another?" (S. James iv. 12.) Do
   not even think unkindly of them, but pray for
   them if they have wronged you: " Pray for

B 2

them which despitefully use you and per-secute you," (S. Matt. v. 44). Do not try and "*spite*" them by mean little tricks, for by so doing you only show yourself to be mean and little. Attend, I pray you, to all this, Because, if you have not Charity you have nothing. "Though I have all faith, so that I could remove mountains, and have not charity, I am nothing." (1 Cor. xii. 2).

I hope you will follow the suggestions here given you, but not only that, if you do these things and any one asks you "What mean ye by this Service?" or, "Why do ye this?" I hope you will be able now to tell them

" THE REASON WHY."

The Parish Tracts.

No. II.

"DO THIS."

This Tract is not intended to be controversial. I leave that to those who have time for controversy. My aim is to place in the hands of earnest enquirers a plain statement of *facts* in regard to the Holy Eucharist. I have, therefore, no views of my own to bring forward, no theories to broach, no prejudices to impose on others. The statements here made as " facts " may be relied on as *certain truth*, as witnessed by the combined testimony of Holy Writ, and the universal consent of the Catholic Church of all ages. If any are offended at what is stated, they would be equally so were I to transcribe word for word several well-known passages on this subject from Holy Scripture. It is now, as always, a " hard saying," (S. John vi. 50), and now, as always, there will be some who " cannot receive it."

FACT I.—The words " Do This," in their literal, grammatical, and doctrinal sense in the Greek Testament mean, " Offer this Sacrifice."

REMARKS: The command was given by our Great High Priest Jesus Christ to the assembly of Apostles the night before His Death. The Sacrifice referred to was the Holy Eucharist, which is offered as a memorial of the one great Sacrifice of Calvary. The obligation to offer it was imposed upon, and accepted, by each member of the Apostolic College. They, in their turn imposed the like obligation, and conferred the necessary powers, upon every Priest ordained by them. The offering of this Sacrifice continually, unceasingly, as the only Divinely appointed office of the Church, is *the Mark* which at once distinguishes a true branch of the Church Catholic from all the innumerable sects and denominations now in existence. The Church of England by imposing on her Priesthood at their ordination this duty, and by providing in her Liturgy for the offering of this Sacrifice at least weekly, accepts, formally and practically, the obligation contained in the Divine words, " Do This."

FACT II.—In the Divine command, " *Do this,*" it is implied, not only that every Priest shall offer this Sacrifice, but that *every Christian shall be a partaker of the Sacrifice.*

REMARKS: It has been already stated, but it may be well repeated, that the act of worship

known to us as Holy Communion was the only
formal Service known to the first Christians.
Preaching was, of course, necessary to proclaim
the truth and bring men over to accept it;
Baptism was then immediately resorted to, to
make them Christians; after which, so necessary was the *individual reception* of the Blessed
Sacrament, that to continue steadfast in "breaking of bread" was from the first recognised as
a test of true Christianity, (Acts ii. 42), to say
nothing of the extreme probability that a Daily
Celebration of the Holy Communion was the
rule in Apostolic days, (Acts ii. 46). If, then,
Holy Scripture is thus emphatic in its testimony to the necessity of believers being Communicants, and if the Church declares this
Sacrament to be " necessary to salvation " (*see
Catechism*), the terrible thought is forced upon
us that if we are living in wilful and habitual
neglect of this means of grace, we are living
outside the covenanted mercies of God! May
God give us grace to realise not only what a
precious privilege is offered to us, but what a
solemn obligation is imposed upon us by those
Divine words, " *Do This.*"

FACT III.—The Presence of Christ in the Sacrament of His Love is a Real Presence.

REMARKS: A word or two only here, for

the subject requires a Tract to itself.* I do not attempt to define the manner of this wondrous Presence, for the Church has not defined it. It does not need that I should, for definitions are hard terms and I write for plain people, and to them I repeat Christ's words, " THIS IS MY BODY," and the Church of England's words, " The Body and Blood of Christ which are VERILY AND INDEED taken and received by the faithful in the Lord's Supper." No words in the English or any other language could be plainer than these. They are sufficient for me, and with thankfulness I accept them. A REAL, glorious, wondrous, mysterious, awful Presence ! and, mark, it is just *this* fact which invests with such vast importance the Divine Command—

"DO THIS."

* See Tract No. xviii., page 69.

The Parish Tracts.

CALVARY.

Throughout all ages of the Church's history, God's holy people have ever found the Passion (or suffering) of Jesus *the* subject above all others which is best fitted to break again the stony heart, and to bring forth anew from the deep fountains of the soul fresh streams of repentance unto Life Eternal. Every tender feeling in the heart of man, woman, or child, is stirred and touched to the quick by a devout contemplation of Jesus on Calvary. It would be unnatural were it otherwise.

But there are times when this subject is forced upon us; times when even those who make no attempt to lead a Christian life, must be reached by some exceptional means, in order that they, too, may be arrested in the midst of their thoughtlessness and earnestly pressed to come aside, if but for a moment, and cast their eyes on this great sight—Jesus on Calvary. Such a time is Passion-tide, by which the Church understands the fourteen days before Easter. Such a time above all others is Good Friday, the awful day on which the shameful deed was done.

Reader! without further preface, I ask you to stop—and behold! the city of Jerusalem is before you. The gilded pinnacles of its gorgeous Temple glitter in the flashing rays of an Eastern sun. That same sun casts its beaming light on Calvary's summit. There is a path, small and rugged, which leads from the City to the top of the mount. Along that path, wearied, footsore, bloodstained, there passeth the God-Man who is about to redeem the world! Yes, bearing His own Cross, mocked and continuously insulted, falling again and again under the cruel weight, toiling and toiling on, Jesus of Nazareth passeth by—up the stony slopes of Calvary!

But the journey is over now. The summit of the mount is reached. The Saviour, exhausted with the inhuman fatigue His enemies have forced Him to undergo, for the last time falls beneath the weight of His heavy burden, and a few brief moments of rest strengthen Him for the further agonies now to be endured. The crowd gathers thick around Him, while rude and vulgar voices shout forth fresh insults, and mocking jibes!

Isaac, the type of Jesus, was laid upon the wood but *not* sacrificed. Jesus is now laid upon the wood of the Cross to *be* sacrificed. A ram in the thicket saved Isaac—no ram to save Jesus! He must die!

His limbs, every muscle aching with the strain of the terrible journey just completed, these limbs are now taken hold of by rough soldiers and fiercely stretched, till they reach the *points of fixture* on the Cross. Now, they strike! The nails shoot through the swollen and tender flesh! shouts of ribald laughter are the only response to the moan of anguish which escapes the lips of the Divine, yet human Sufferer; and then, the cross is raised, the victim is exposed, and in the midst of His writhing agony, He is able to breathe forth the loving prayer—"Father, forgive them, for they know not what they do!" The end approaches. The Disciples gather under the dark shadow of the Cross. The holy Maries are there; the loved Disciple, S. John, is there; these, with others, watch with throbbing hearts and scalding tears the last hours of Jesus on Calvary!

Dear Reader! you cannot but be moved by this "Story of the Cross"—this terrible story of Calvary. A great deal is said in these days of a "personal Saviour"; "Jesus died for *me*" is on the lips of many a one at all seasons of the year. But do you realise that these awful sufferings of which we have here spoken were really endured not only *for you*, but on account of *your* sins? Do you believe the fact that your own sins were part of the weight that crushed the life out of the Son of God on Calvary? Ah! if you speak henceforth of a "*personal Saviour*," remember, I pray you, that you have have had a hand in that murder of the righteous Man ;—" He was bruised for OUR iniquities," (Isaiah liii. 5). Let this story, then, bring you on your knees in penitence. Repent you of your past sins, and implore that crucified Saviour to have mercy on *you*. Make it a personal matter by all means. That will be your best security.

Perhaps this Tract will be placed in your hands in time to influence your conduct on GOOD FRIDAY. If so, what shall be your resolve? To make a holiday of that day? Oh, surely not! I cannot believe that you will make merry with the unbelieving world on the day of your Lord's Death. Surely you will spend much of it in prayer and meditation. In your homes, and while mixing with others, let your quiet demeanour show that you are sensible of its being no ordinary day, no common event, which is being commemorated. I pray you, make a devout use of whatever Services are provided for you, and bear in mind the specially solemn character which belongs to the three last hours of the Redeemer's agony, viz., **12** to **3.** Let the darkness which overshadowed the earth during that time overshadow your soul also, and go, spend those three dread hours, at least, with Jesus on

CALVARY.

The Parish Tracts.

No. IV.

THE DYING AND THE DEAD.

Reader! you cannot be unfamiliar with Death. It visits every household—and, sooner or later, every member of every household. It will one day visit *you* and clasp you in its cold embrace. But before you become yourself a victim to this "last enemy" it may well happen that some one else within the circle of your influence may receive the solemn message—"Prepare to meet thy God." In either of these cases, whether as regards yourself, or some member of your family, I hope that this Tract will be useful in bringing to your notice certain matters of much importance, though, alas! too often neglected in our treatment of the dying and the dead.

I.—And first it must be above all things necessary that the dying member of Christ's fold should be strengthened with every available means of grace which the Church offers him. The Church of England provides two Offices for this purpose, the "Visitation" and the "Communion" of the sick; and I desire to draw special attention to the fact that the Visitation

Office is appointed to come first. Alas! this beautiful Service is too often omitted owing to the priest not being sent for till the sick person is *too weak in body and mind to take his part in it.* If you will look at the rubrics of the Prayer Book you will see that the hardest part of the work in this Service falls to the lot of the sick person. He is to be "*moved to make a special confession of his sins if he feel his conscience troubled with any weighty matter.*" Now, if a dying Christian is sincere, it is certain that all sin will appear to him in the light of a "weighty matter," and it is, therefore, most important that before departing this life he should, at least, be offered this means of grace which the Church provides; but I maintain that he will be utterly unfit to take his part in it unless he still retains full possession of his mental faculties. If he is in a state of great weakness, it is hopeless to expect him to be able to open up his past life before God's servant, and he may thus lose the "benefit of absolution" which he has "humbly and heartily desired." I do not say—God forbid— that he will die unforgiven. God *can* pardon sin without the ordinary means of grace being used at all; but I do say that, as God has chosen to give "power, and commandment, to his Ministers to declare and pronounce to his people, being penitent, the Absolution and

Remission of their sins,"* the dying Churchman ought to be invited to receive this means of grace to his soul's health, before his sickness has become " almost unto death." Therefore, in all cases of serious illness, see that a Priest of the Church is at once sent for, and do not wait, as is so often done, till the sickness is pronounced a " hopeless case."

II.—And now, dear reader, I will suppose that all has been done that is possible both for the bodily and spiritual welfare of your loved one, and that the time has come for you to bear up under the great trial of bereavement. The sickness has been indeed " unto death "; the last breath has been drawn—your dear one is no more ! I pray you now to remember :—

1. That this Body, now a corpse, will rise again.
2. That the soul of that person is still alive. (See Note.)

In arranging the body for interment, therefore, you will act throughout as if you realised these great truths. Let the body be washed not by hirelings, but by the more tender and loving hands of friends. Let the arms be folded over the breast, and not ex-

---

* Church of England Prayer Book.

NOTE.—By this I mean that the soul in Paradise (1) is conscious of its own existence ; (2) has an interest in the spiritual welfare of those still alive in the flesh ; (3) is able to feel pleasure or pain. This much concerning the condition of the departed is certain from the story of Dives and Lazarus.

tended down the sides. In the death-chamber let a small table be placed at the foot of the bed to serve as a stand for a cross and two candles, these latter to be kept burning night and day till the hour of interment arrives, as a sign of the light into which the departed soul has passed. In arranging for burial, do not seek unduly to preserve the body by coffins of lead or oak, or by the use of brick vaults. The law of God is "Dust thou art and unto dust thou shalt return." Do not attempt to interfere with the natural process of decay. A coffin of elm is the best and simplest. A long cross of metal, or white wood, stretching downwards, the whole length of the coffin is recommended. At the funeral do not make use of a hearse, paid "bearers," black scarfs, or hatbands. These are more suitable for the funeral of a Pagan or an Infidel than that of a Christian. Most important of all, ask the parish clergyman to have a celebration of Holy Communion, either at the same time, and as part of the Funeral Service, or earlier the same day. In either case the body will, of course, be brought into the Church, the friends of the deceased will receive Communion, and when the Church Militant Prayer is read, in which the faithful departed are commemorated, then remember the soul which has fled, and ask God to have mercy on its shortcomings, and to grant that it may rest in peace. Thus will you have shown your love for the **DYING,** and your reverence for the **DEAD.**

The Parish Tracts.

No. V.
HOLY THURSDAY.

Amidst all the sad divisions of Christendom it is easy to see one thing which distinguishes the false from the true; there is one broad line which must for ever separate imperfect systems of religion from the one true Faith. The distinction is this: all systems of religion outside the Church are more or less religious of sentiment, by which I mean that they make salvation to depend *on the feelings of the believer;* whereas the Catholic Faith teaches that our salvation depends on certain great FACTS which have taken place, and which cannot be affected by our individual feelings. Thus, an imperfectly taught Christian will say, "I have that within me which tells me that I am one of the saved;" whereas one properly instructed will say, "If I am hereafter saved it will be because I have faithfully proclaimed my belief in all the great facts of our redemption through Christ Jesus." The religion of the one must therefore consist to a large extent in a continuous excitement of the feelings, to bring them to the supposed necessary pitch of devotion; whereas the religion of

c

the true Churchman consists in a continuous commemoration of the great facts to which he owes his
only chance of salvation.

Reader! you will already have perceived my
motive in pointing out this distinction between the
teaching of the Church and all other systems of
religion. ASCENSION DAY is close upon us.
On that day we shall be called upon to go in spirit
to Mount Olivet, and bear our testimony to the
final triumph of the Risen Saviour. Now this great
festival has suffered from a strange and unpardonable
neglect, which were unaccountable but for what I
have said above. That, however, explains it all.
People have wandered away from Jesus to themselves!
They have centred their religion in their own feelings,
instead of placing all their hopes in what Christ has
done.   And in proportion as they have done this,
the observance of Holy Days has become more and
more lax, even amongst professing Church people.

Now, in regard to Ascension Day, I desire to
point out that its importance and rank as a festival
is not a matter of opinion at all. Its position is
fixed for us, in a manner which admits of no question,
by the fact that it is one of those five great festivals
for which a proper Preface is provided in the Communion Service of our Prayer Book. Only two
week days in the whole year are thus distinguished.
The one is Christmas Day ; the other is Ascension
Day, or Holy Thursday.

Why the feast of our Lord's Ascension has been

thus honoured is easy to understand. This act of His—this return in triumph to His Father's Home—was the completion of His work. Without it, that work would have been unfinished, and therefore incomplete. The very Church itself which Christ had founded could have no organised existence till it had received the promised baptism of fire; which, in its turn, could not be given till Christ " sat at the right hand of God." Jesus had indeed died for our sins, and risen again for our justification, but even that was not sufficient. One thing more was necessary. There must be a Mediator between God and man, and that Mediator must plead before the very throne of God the works which He had done to redeem mankind. So Christ "ascended into Heaven," and thanks to that Ascension, "If any man sin we have an ADVOCATE with the Father, Jesus Christ the righteous; and He is the propitiation for our sins." (1 S. John 2, 1.)

God be praised, dear reader, if this little tract should help you to see more clearly these great truths, and so lead you to honour with such honour as is due one of the neglected feasts of our holy Mother Church. I ask you not to be partaker of other people's sins. To omit the due observance of a holy day is to profane that day; and to profane a holy day is a sin. Therefore, do not commit this sin of neglect on the approaching bright festival of our dear Lord's sweet Ascension.

Finally, let the Scripture account of the wondrous event point out to you at once your duty and your privilege.

I. YOUR DUTY.—When the Apostles saw their Lord departing from them, they paid Him the tribute of adoration. "And they WORSHIPPED Him, and returned to Jerusalem with great joy." (S. Luke xxiv, 52.) So will the devout Christian hasten on this "illustrious and refulgent day*" to adore his Lord and his God;—Yes! the Church distinctly calls us all to the Altar on Ascension Day, and there can we best pay our tribute of adoration.

II. YOUR PRIVILEGE.—It was while engaged in blessing His disciples that Christ was taken from them. "And it came to pass, while He blessed them, He was parted from them, and carried up into heaven." (S. Luke xxiv. 51.) So will a special blessing fall on every faithful disciple of Jesus who will go out with Him in spirit to Bethany and to Olivet, and there, on this great and holy festival, "in heart and mind thither ascend," where He has gone before.

"Even he that hath clean hands, and a pure heart, * * * he shall receive the Blessing from the Lord."

Psalm xxiv. 4, 5.

---

* S. Chrysostom.

The Parish Tracts.

"WORKING MEN."

This paper is intended for circulation amongst Working Men. By "Working Men" I mean not only those who labour for a daily, weekly, or monthly wage, but all who are in any way actively engaged in human toil. The tradesman, the peasant farmer, the artisan, the fisherman, the collier, or the miner—all these, and others not specified, are equally with the agricultural labourer included in my mind under the title which heads this tract.

Now, my dear friends, I have a word for you. You live in a busy age; an age when men's minds are no less active than their bodies; in fact, an age of *thought*, an age of WORK. Whether he wills it or no, the working man finds himself forced in these days to make his existence felt, and his voice heard in the settlement of all great questions, whether political, social, or religious. No party in the state, no social reformers, no religious denomination can now afford to dispense with the support and influence of the great class of which I am writing. In saying this, it is far from my desire to flatter the working man. It is no credit to him that he happens to belong to a body of his fellow-creatures which *must*, by its very extensiveness, exercise a considerable influence on human affairs.   It only becomes a credit to him *if he uses this influence aright*, and to help him to do this is my present object.

My working friend,—whoever you are, wherever you live, or whatever may be the special nature of your calling,—you are surrounded by a number of different religious denominations, each of which is equally eager to claim your support.   Each would like to "convert" you and enroll you as a "member" of their sect.   I am equally anxious, for your own sake, as well as on public grounds, that you should give your entire and unwavering support — not to any denomination, but to the CHURCH of your FATHERS.   In the fold of the CHURCH you find rest; for her doctrines are not the speculations of men, but the certain revelations of Divine truth.   In her you will find what you can find nowhere else, the Sacraments of the Gospel, without which you can have no assurance of salvation, but by the devout use of which you will certainly find both pardon and peace.   In her you will find, those sevenfold gifts of the Spirit which are necessary for your spiritual life, and which you cannot expect to receive, except through the appointed channel of Episcopal laying on of hands in the sacred Rite of Confirmation.

So far I have spoken only of your spiritual life. But every man has, as it were, two lives—the Outer Life and the Inner Life, and these two should always correspond and work in harmony with one another. Now, your inner life is that to which I have referred above; your outer life is that part which you take in working, in association with others, for the good of any cause which you may support. For instance, as regards "Temperance," your inner life would be that known only to a small circle—your abstinence from drink; your outer life would be that work which you would do for the advance of the cause in public.

Now I do not see why the Church should not claim your outer life, as well as your inner or spiritual life. If you once learn to love the Church as your Mother, you will surely be anxious to do something for her public good. You are a "Working Man," why not do some WORK for the Church? If you ask me, "What am I to do?"—it is not my business to answer that question, unless you are in my parish. Go to your parish clergyman —say you want to do *something* in a public way for the Church. If he can find nothing for you to do, I am sorry for both him and his parish. I cannot myself, however, imagine such a case to exist. At all events, in nine cases out of ten you will, I am sure, find a hearty welcome from him who is your spiritual father. He is your best earthly friend though you may not think it, and few parishes in England are so small but that there is plenty of room for every earnest Church worker.

If, however, the circumstances are such that you cannot find any work directly under the parish priest, you can still do some work for the Church at large, and most probably for the benefit of your own parish. You can *organize*, and, acting along with others of the same mind as yourself, form a Society or Association having for its object the general interests of the Church.

Many who read this are aware that a " Working Men's Society," in connection with the Church of England, was started some years ago, with its head quarters in London, and branches scattered over the country. I wish that every village as well as every town in which there are even a dozen faithful sons of the Church, had a branch of this Society in its midst. No better way of helping the Church's work could be devised, and if any earnest Church-man who reads this paper desires to act in the spirit of my advice, I can only urge him to join at once the " Church of England Working Men's Society," and, if possible, to forward the founding of new branches wherever one does not already exist. The headquarters of the Society are at 3, Tavistock Street, Covent Garden, Strand, and within the far reaching borders of this Society there is a noble sphere of usefulness for any amount of honest Church-loving

" WORKING MEN."

The Parish Tracts.

No. VII.
DAILY SERVICE.

—

I do not think it can be too often or too plainly stated that according to the rule and discipline of the Church of England, every Priest who holds a cure of souls is in duty bound to conduct a daily Service in the church in which he ministers. When, some thirty or forty years ago, this devout practice began to be revived, some good people affected great astonishment, and wondered "what next" was going to be introduced into their "dear old churches," &c. Since that time many things which in those days would have appeared strange have not only been introduced, but are now demanded by the people themselves, and this habit of asking for their rights, which is becoming more and more common amongst the laity, is in every way to be encouraged. What is called the principle of "levelling up," that is *raising the general tone of the parish*, is often dependent on the public spirit which animates the parishioners. The clergyman is perhaps afraid to make any so-called "innovations;" he would much like this or that, but he is afraid he would not be supported by his flock. Many clergy are in this position, and it is just in such a case that it is the duty of the parishioner to step in and *ask* for such privileges as the Church prescribes.

Perhaps this Tract may find its way into some parish in which there is *no daily Service.* And yet, in that parish, be it large or small, there are doubtless some few souls who would greatly value such means of grace. If so, my dear reader, your course is clear. If you can satisfy yourself that even a literal " two or three " would be willing daily to " gather to-gether " to take part in Matins or Evensong, you need have no hesitation in respectfully approaching your Parish Priest, and drawing his attention to the following law, or " Rubric," in the Book of Common Prayer :—

" And all Priests and Deacons are to say DAILY the Morning and Evening Prayer * * *. And the Curate that ministereth in every parish Church or Chapel, being at home, and not being otherwise reasonably hindered, shall say the same in the parish Church or Chapel where he ministereth, and shall cause a bell to be tolled thereunto a convenient time before he begin, that the people may come to hear God's Word, and to pray with him."

In that Rubric is enshrined at once the clergyman's *duty* and the people's *right*. In other, and yet plainer words, if in any parish daily Service is not provided, it is within the rights of the parishioners, or any number of them, to request that in this matter the undoubted law of the Church shall be complied with.

So far, I have written simply as an impartial member of the Chnrch of England, but I now write as a Priest of that Church, and point, not without a feeling of sorrow and disappointment, to the other side of the question. This Tract will doubtless also find its way into many parishes where there *is* a daily Service, which Service, however, is *not adequately supported by the congregation.* This, I grieve to say, is the general experience of those Clergy who are determined to do their duty through good report and evil report. They do provide the appointed Services, but find themselves too often compelled to minister in almost empty Churches. In a word, the people *do not come !* My dear friend, " these things ought not so to be." Granted, that it is the duty and privilege of the Parish Priest to go to his Church twice every day, and there recite his daily Office, even if he says it in the ears of God alone, this does not annul or do away with that part of the Rubric which directs a bell to be tolled in order " that *the people may come* to hear God's Word, and to pray with him.

Now, of one thing I feel certain, and that is this —that if you can only be brought to see this matter in its proper light, so that you shall recognize it as a duty to support the *principle* of daily Service, then I believe that notwithstanding any difficulties in your way, you will become at least an occasional, if not a frequent attendant at the week-day Services in your

Church. And I feel no less certain that if you are sincerely attached to the Church of England, and earnestly desire to grow in grace, to become less worldly, and more holy, you will find a regular habit of occasional attendance at such Services, not only most helpful to you in a spiritual sense, but a source of ever-increasing pleasure and interest.

I will conclude with a word of practical advice. If a daily Service is provided for you, in your parish, and you feel moved from reading this paper to attend such Service, though you may not hitherto have done so, begin by making a rule to attend ONCE every week, and *fix a day* as most convenient to your home life, for such attendance. Just think what a difference there would be in the daily Services if this plan were generally adopted! Every day would see gathered together a nice compact little congregation—not composed always of the same faithful half-dozen or so, as perhaps is the rule at present, but made up almost each day of different persons who had their own fixed day for attending such or such a Service. Until some such plan as this is adopted I fear that most parishes will continue to labour under the present almost universal difficulty of getting together a reasonable number of attendants at

"DAILY SERVICE."

The Parish Tracts.

CONVERSION.

The fact that Conversion is everywhere talked and written about is of itself a proof that it is a subject which has an absorbing interest for multitudes. Its vast importance fully justifies its being thus thrust into the very foreground of all religious controversy. No sect or denomination but has its own peculiar views as to what constitutes conversion. And what wonder that the religious passions and emotions of every age in the history of Christianity have been stirred to the quick by a subject of which our Lord himself has said, "Except ye be converted ye shall not enter into the Kingdom of Heaven." I purpose, then, to consider—

I.—WHAT CONVERSION IS.

II.—WHAT CONVERSION IS NOT.

I. WHAT CONVERSION IS.

1. The first stage or sign of approaching conversion consists in the sinner being deeply afflicted with a consciousness of his past sins, and of his present sinful state. In some cases this consciousness

of sin comes suddenly, as for instance, when one whose past life has been extremely wicked is all at once led to see the error of his ways. But in the case of Christians who have been carefully trained in the way they should go from childhood, and who have continued firm in their spiritual relations with Christ and His Church through the Sacraments, no sudden change is to be expected. The consciousness of sin has grown gradually stronger within them year after year, so that they have passed on to the after stages of conversion without experiencing any violent or sudden awakening to their state of guilt. And even should any Christian experience such a sudden awakening as we have described, this change of disposition is in no case to be mistaken for conversion itself. As well might the " little cloud " of Mount Carmel have been mistaken for the refreshing rain which followed. If, then, you are smitten with a deep sense of guilt, and are determined to amend your ways, this is not conversion—but it is a very hopeful sign. " Behold there ariseth a little cloud out of the sea, like a man's hand !" (1 Kings xviii. 44.)

2. The second stage of conversion consists in the confession or acknowledgment of your sins, and in receiving the cleansing which God vouchsafes to all who " lay their sins at Jesu's feet."

Here it is important to note that not your " sin " only but your *sins* are to be confessed. To cry aloud and declare yourself a sinner is not enough.

Even Judas the Betrayer knew better than that, for in his confession (which alas! was without true repentance, and therefore useless), even he confessed the particular sin which then lay upon his conscience. "I have sinned *in that I have betrayed the innocent blood.*" So must the contrite sinner who is being converted "examine himself" that he may discover in detail the sins of his past life, and confess them.

And then he must be cleansed. As the leprosy of Naaman, the Syrian, was literally " washed away" in the waters of Jordan, so must the leprosy of your sins, dear reader, be actually "washed away" by the cleansing of the Sacraments which Christ has left in His Church for that purpose. Of course I know not which Sacrament or means of grace is your special need just now. But whether it be Baptism, or Absolution, or the Holy Communion, sure I am that in either of these you may find the true waters of Jordan for the washing of your soul, so that it shall become again like unto the soul of a little child.

3. And lastly, if you are to be truly converted, you must produce *fruit in your life.* "Every tree that bringeth not forth good fruit is hewn down, and cast into the fire," (S. Matt. vii. 12). In other words, you must show forth by your *works* that you are not only called to a new life, but that you are in every spiritual sense a " new creature," walking constantly in the fear of God, and having your

soul frequently strengthened and refreshed by the dew of Christ's Sacramental grace; for "Faith without works is dead "—(S. James ii. 26)—and you know of One who has told you to "Let your light so shine before men that they may see your *good works*, and glorify your Father which is in Heaven," (S. Matt. v. 16).

And now it only remains for me to warn you against false theories of conversion which Satan has caused to be proclaimed through the lips of false prophets so that he may destroy, if possible, " the very elect." Consider, then,

II.—WHAT CONVERSION IS NOT.

It is not this :—A terrible conviction of being in a lost state, accompanied by a violent wrenching of the emotions and despair of being saved. This followed, more or less speedily, by an " assurance " that you are after all one of God's elect, and are consequently in a position not only to relate your own " experience " for the edification of others, but authorised, if you choose, to minister the Gospel to perishing souls. That, in a word, you have suddenly emerged from a state of darkness to a condition of light, that you are in no danger of falling into further sin, that you can, in consequence, live without the life-giving power of Sacramental grace : that, in fact, you are " converted," and therefore " saved !" Dear reader, believe me, that is NOT

CONVERSION.

The Parish Tracts.

CHURCH OR CHAPEL.

I address myself, in this Tract, to all who " profess and call themselves Christians," and who, as a token of their Christian profession, are agreed that it is their bounden duty "not to forsake the assembling of ourselves together," (Heb. x. 25), but to meet at stated times, and at least every Sunday, in some " place of worship," for the purpose of prayer, praise, and edification by the hearing and preaching of the Word of God. Every denomination of Christians is so far agreed in the objects of their public assemblies, while a large number are further agreed as to the desirableness of receiving, at the hands of their appointed ministers, certain means of grace, such as Baptism and the " Communion of the Body and Blood of Christ," (1 Cor. x. 16). Now, when you consider the vast number of different religious bodies who meet together every week for these most sacred objects, it must be a matter of great importance for each Christian to decide to which of these innumerable societies he

D

will attach himself.   Shall he belong to the Church
of his fathers, or shall he join some society of Christians, who from one cause or another have separated
themselves from the Church?   Shall he join in old
prayers, litanies, Psalms, and " spiritual songs,"
which have been continuously used for hundreds of
years, or shall he go from place to place ever seeking, like the Athenians of old, to " hear some new
thing?" (Acts xvii. 21.)   Shall he be a Churchman
or a Nonconformist?   Shall he, in a word, go to
Church, or go to *Chapel?*

In order to simplify the case, let me first impress
upon you that practically there are only two alter-
natives.   The one is *the Church*, the other is
separation from the Church.   If, as one of the Baptized, you cut yourself off from full communion with
the mystical Body of Christ, this is *separation*, and
it can matter but little to which sect or denomination of the Baptized you adhere.   The Wesleyans,
Congregationalists, Baptists, Methodists, Quakers,
Jumpers, Christadelphians, Testament Disciples,
Salvation Army, or Presbyterians, all these, and a
hundred others I might name, are so far agreed in
what they themselves consider as essentials, that
the difference between them amounts to nothing
more than a matter of taste or habit.   If you to-day
belong to the one, you may change your " place of
worship " each succeeding Sunday.   You will find
in each such assembly a form of worship so closely

resembling the other that the amount of edification you receive will depend, not on the name of the sect whose meeting-house you attend, but on the ability which the pastor of that place possesses. My whole anxiety, therefore, is concerned with the one great question—CHURCH or "CHAPEL."

Now, is there any one thing, easily seen, which so completely distinguishes these two great branches of religious belief, that a professing Christian can at once decide which is ·the haven of safety where he would be? There is, dear fellow-Christian; the difference between Church and Chapel briefly summed up is this: the Church depends for her very life on what is called the Sacramental System, and which I will presently explain; the Chapel rejects the Sacramental System, and depends for its life on the amount of interest which is evinced in the "preaching of the Word." The Church insists on Sacraments as being "necessary to salvation," and therefore provides that every child shall receive the Sacrament of Baptism (S. John iii. 5), and every adult the Sacrament of Christ's Body and Blood, (S. John vi. 53). The Chapel teaches that Baptism and the Breaking of Bread are merely edifying ordinances, good enough in their way, but in no sense necessary to the salvation of the sinner's soul. The Church, therefore, places Sacraments before preaching, as far as believers are concerned; the Chapel places preaching before Sacraments. It is,

therefore, a very common thing to hear Dissenters
say of Churchpeople—"They put Sacraments in
the place of Christ." I hope no Churchman would
be so uncharitable as to say what would, however,
be quite as true, " Dissenters put preaching in the
place of Christ." No! I do not believe that
either Church or Chapel people commit this error.
They both desire to believe in Christ and to live in
Him ; but they differ as to the means by which this
belief is to be expressed, and this life to be commu-
nicated to the soul. In fact, as I said, the system
of the Church is Sacramental; the system of the
Chapel is non-Sacramental.

Now, there can be no greater mistake than to
suppose, as alas ! many do, that it "does not
matter" which you believe in—Church or Chapel.
You cannot believe in both, and the object of
this Tract is simply to urge on every earnest
Christian to be " fully persuaded in his own mind,"
as to which of the two systems I have described is
most in accordance with Scripture ; and I think that
a careful and candid examination of the texts I have
indicated will be sufficient to settle the minds of
most of my readers as to which has the strongest
claims on his support,

CHURCH OR CHAPEL.

The Parish Tracts.

No. X.

CONFIRMATION.

The Sacramental Rite of Confirmation is deliberately placed by the Church of England in a position of importance which is scarcely inferior to the position assigned to the two "Sacraments of the Gospel"—Holy Baptism and Holy Communion. This will be seen at a glance by anyone who bears in mind these two simple facts :—1. In the Catechism it is stated that the Sacrament of the Lord's Supper is "*necessary to salvation.*" 2. At the end of the Confirmation Service it is ordered that "none be admitted to the Holy Communion, *until such time as he be confirmed,* or be ready and desirous to be confirmed." It is plain, then, that regarding the matter from the Prayer Book point of view, Confirmation is itself a sacred ordinance of the Church which is, under ordinary circumstances, necessary for our salvation ; while for circumstances which are not ordinary, it is provided that a desire and readiness to receive the rite may be considered sufficient to entitle the Christian to the privileges of Communion. Now let us see what may be fairly gathered from Holy Writ as to this means of grace.

I will content myself with one single passage, namely
Acts viii. 14-17 :—

"When the Apostles which were at Jerusalem heard that Samaria
had received the Word of God, they sent unto them Peter and
John; who, when they were come down, prayed for them that they
might receive the Holy Ghost (for as yet he was fallen upon none
of them; only they were baptized in the name of the Lord Jesus).
Then laid they their hands on them, and they received the Holy
Ghost."

Here I find the rite of Confirmation most plainly described under the same title by which it is known
in our own Church, viz., the " laying on of hands,"
and from this single passage of Scripture it is
certain—

1. That there was such a rite in the earliest
Apostolic times.

2. That this rite was administered only by the
Apostles; that is to say, by ministers holding the
rank of Bishops.

3. That those only were confirmed who had
already been baptized.

4. That the object of the laying on of hands was,
as it still is, to convey the Holy Ghost.

Whether we turn, therefore, to the Bible or the
Prayer Book, we must be equally convinced, if we
are sincere Christians, that wilfully to neglect Confirmation must be a grave, if not fatal, error; and
this conviction will surely lead us to seek the very
earliest opportunity of removing this reproach, either
by going ourselves or leading others to the stream
of living water which still flows fresh and limpid

from the Rock which is Christ: " Ho, every one that thirsteth, come ye to the waters, (Isaiah lv. 1).

Now let me suppose, dear reader, two things :— 1. That there is going to be a Confirmation held shortly in your neighbourhood. 2. That you are *not yet confirmed.* Shall I urge you to *go,* or shall I implore you to *stay away?* Remember that great numbers present themselves for Confirmation who had far better postpone the matter. And I would take this means of placing before you the circumstances under which I should NOT advise you, at present, to be confirmed. Bearing in mind that, when the Bishop's hands are laid on you, you will receive the seven gifts of the Holy Ghost for the express purpose of impressing upon your soul the " seal " of the Lord, (Eph. i. 13), and thereby giving to your soul a *character* or fitness to feed on Christ's Body and Blood, I would implore you to *stay away* from Confirmation—(1.) If you are living in the habitual indulgence of any great sin which you do not intend to break off—sins, for example, against the seventh commandment, or swearing, drunkenness and the like; (2.) If it is your intention (as it is of so many who go to be confirmed) to continue after Confirmation to absent yourself from the Sacrament of the Altar. In either of these cases I pray you not to make a mockery of this holy rite by receiving the outward sign, when you have no intention of profiting by the inward grace received.

But with regard to many who read this Tract, I hope I may with confidence urge you to *go*. And you will go in a proper spirit, and with a right intention. You will, in the first place, be regular and punctual in attendance at whatever means of instruction are provided for you. You will, during the time of your preparation, "pray without ceasing;" you will resolve by God's grace to overcome the sin that so easily, aye! and alas, so frequently besets you; you will not only with your lips but in your heart, with sincerity and truth, "renew the solemn promise and vow that was made in your name at your Baptism;" and, lastly, you will go with this one solemn thought ever present to your mind, namely, that your body is about to become a tabernacle for the most sacred Flesh and Blood of Jesus, God-Incarnate! Oh! what a tremendous responsibility is this! Yet, dear fellow Christian, what a glorious privilege! God offers you these abundant means of grace in His Church on earth to fit you for a place in His Church Triumphant in Heaven. He endues this Church and the Priests thereof with spiritual powers, so that, from the cradle to the grave, you need lack nothing; He feeds you in green pastures, and ever leads you forth beside fresh waters of comfort. And He Who is the COMFORTER offers to come to you now in

CONFIRMATION.

The Parish Tracts.

No. XI.

HOLY BAPTISM.

I. The Case of Adults, or Grown Persons.

Are you, my reader, baptized? and if not, why not? I hear you answer in some such words as these:—"My parents, for some reason or other, omitted to have me baptized when I was a child, and for myself I have never troubled about the matter. I know many very good persons who are in a like case with myself, so I do not see why I should be more concerned than they. Besides, I have heard many preachers declare that 'Sacraments cannot save us,' and I am, therefore, encouraged in my indifference. I really do not see that Baptism can do me any good." Alas! such language is too common, for the ignorance about this Sacrament is fearful. Now, I am addressing you, my unbaptized friend, and I pray you to hear and ponder calmly on what I say; Holy Baptism has for eighteen hundred years been regarded by the whole Church throughout the world as a means of grace which is NECESSARY for every single soul. We have nothing to do, at present, with the case of the heathen, or of those who lose the privilege of Baptism through no fault of their own. We leave these to the uncovenanted mercies of God, knowing that in this, as in all matters, " the Judge of all the earth shall do right." Your case, my friend, is not the same as theirs. You live in the full blaze of Gospel light; the Sacraments are not kept from you, they are pressed upon your acceptance; you cannot plead ignorance any longer, for I do now most solemnly declare to you, that if you are now unbaptized, and die in that condition, you die wilfully rejecting the express terms of salvation as declared by Christ Himself. " He that believeth *and is baptized* shall be saved ;" (S. Mark xvi. 26.) and again, " Except a man be BORN OF WATER and of the Spirit, he cannot enter into the Kingdom of God," (S. John iii. 5) ; and I ask you to notice how the Church insists on this latter passage as decisive in the matter, for, in the office of " Baptism of such as are of Riper Years," the Prayer Book says, " Beloved, ye hear in this Gospel the express words of our Saviour Christ, that except a man be born of water and of the Spirit he cannot enter into the Kingdom of God. *Whereby ye may perceive the great necessity of this Sacrament*, where it may be had." Here then, dear friend, you have both Scripture and Prayer Book urging you not to imperil your soul by neglecting what the great Head of the Church, Jesus Christ Himself, has declared to be needful for our salvation. Your duty, then, is clear. At once seek the help of some clergyman of the Church, and

ask him to help you to prepare for Holy Baptism.
Remember, " Now is the accepted time." Another
delay, and you may be TOO LATE.

II.—THE CASE of INFANTS.

The neglect of Infant Baptism arises from three
causes :—

1. The Anabaptist heresy. 2. The indifference
of irreligious parents. 3. The ignorance of many
parents as to the importance of Holy Baptism.

It is only those who come under the last head that
I can hope to influence, by referring them to

(1) The Scripture Warrant
    for, and   } INFANT BAPTISM.
(2) The Church's Teach-
    ing as to

First, then, as regards the Scripture warrant, I
remark that it is especially stated in several places
of Scripture that ALL persons are to be baptized,
and unless there can be found any passage of Holy
Writ which *excludes* infants from this rite, it must
be conceded that they are rightly made partakers of
it. I will give only two quotations to bear out my
statement that all are to be baptized. 1. S. Peter,
addressing a multitude of people on the day of Pente-
cost, says:—"Repent, and be baptized *every one of you*
* * * for the promise is to you *and to your*
children." (Acts ii. 38 and 39.) 2. When the
jailor of Philippi was converted, we are told he
" was baptized, he *and all his*, straightway ;" (Acts

xvi. 33); "*all his*" plainly meaning all his family. It is, therefore, certain by the Word of God that children ought to be baptized.

Secondly, as to the Church's teaching on this matter, this also is very plain. The Church specially provides a Service in her Prayer Book for the "Public Baptism of Infants," and for this reason:—When we are born into this world we are born in sin, "children of wrath;" that is to say, we are born subject to God's wrath on account of the sin of Adam which we inherit from him. In order to cleanse us from this sinful condition, Christ has provided the Sacrament of Holy Baptism, whereby we are "regenerated"—that is, born again—and made members of Him and children of God. This is called the doctrine of "Baptismal Regeneration," and is formally expressed by the Church in these words, spoken by the priest immediately after the Baptism of the child,—"Seeing now, dearly beloved brethren, that this child IS REGENERATE, and grafted into the body of Christ's Church, let us give thanks unto Almighty God for these benefits."

If, then, this Tract should fall into the hands of any parents who have children *not yet baptized*, I solemnly call upon them, in the name of God, to make immediate arrangements with some duly-ordained minister of the Church that these children may be "born again" in the sacred waters of

HOLY BAPTISM.

The Parish Tracts.

JUDGMENT TO COME.

This Tract is put into your hands, dear friend, to try and help you to realise in some measure the terrible fact contained in those words of Scripture:—"It is appointed unto men once to die, but after this THE JUDGMENT" (Hebrews ix. 27). I call it a terrible fact, because it will doubtless prove to be so to the vast majority of the human race. To all who have lived without God in the world, or who are at this moment living in that state, the fact that, as the prophet Joel puts it, "The day of the Lord cometh," is a fact full of unspeakable terror. You may be indifferent to this fact, but you cannot escape its consequences. You may defy God all your life with apparent impunity, and cling to the Atheist's hope —the only hope he has, poor soul—that death is the end of human existence, and that it is, therefore, a matter of little consequence how you live, or how you die; but you cannot alter the FACT that at a certain hour of a certain day, which " no man knoweth," the Lord shall come from Heaven with mighty power and great glory, "with ten thousand of His Saints, to execute JUDGMENT upon all, and to convince all that are ungodly among them of all their ungodly deeds which they have ungodly committed." (S. Jude, 14 and 15).

It is this terrible COMING of the Son of God that we have in our minds when we think or speak of His ADVENT, and, in order to mark the great importance of this most solemn subject, the Church has, as you know, set apart a special season of nearly four weeks' duration before Christmas Day for its particular consideration.   During those weeks of Advent the Church calls her children to withdraw as much as possible from the pleasures of the world, in order that they may give more time to prayer, and to the contemplation of this and other kindred subjects ; and, if we are faithful sons and daughters of our spiritual mother, the Church, I doubt not we shall gladly avail ourselves year by year of this special opportunity to ponder on the awful thought of JUDGMENT TO COME.   But the subject is one, dear reader, which demands *immediate consideration* on your part, if you have not already weighed its terrific import.   This Tract may reach you at a time of year when Advent is still far distant.   Do not, for your soul's sake, say that you will postpone the matter till that season comes round again !   I pray you, let not a day pass till you have done all you know to commence a serious preparation for that

sure and terrible Judgment which shall certainly one
day overtake you in common with all mankind, for
" we shall all stand before the Judgment-seat of
Christ." (Rom. xiv. 10.) Ask yourself candidly,
" Am I ready to pass through this fierce ordeal?
To stand one amidst millions of souls, and, *before
them all*, confess and be judged for every unrepented
sin I have ever committed? Am I ready to face the
frown of my outraged God?—His face once radiant
with mercy, now clouded over with just anger; His
eyes, once beaming with compassionate love, now
fixed on me with a piercing glance of outraged
justice, ready to pass upon me, if found guilty, the
dread unalterable sentence, 'Depart from me, ye
cursed, into everlasting fire.' (S. Matt. xxv. 41)—
Am I prepared for this? Shall I be able to stand
before the great white throne whereon sitteth the
' Judge of all the earth?' Shall I have the courage
to turn my head and gaze upon that mighty sea of
faces, some indeed glowing with the light of innocence, reflected upon them by Him in whom they
trusted, the Sun of Righteousness, but others, yea,
the vast majority, weeping and wailing at the
thought of the mercy which they have rejected,
the long threatened judgment which they despised?
Shall I be able to meet the fierce glance of the
enemy of souls, Satan, the great " accuser of his
brethren," who shall come forward to bear his terrible
witness against his victims? Shall I be able to gain-

say his accusation, that I fell before his temptations, that I committed the sins to which he allured me, that I did, alas! delay till too late my repentance? Shall I be able to meet the sadly solemn countenance of my guardian angel who shall likewise come forward and bear witness how he strove to protect me and keep me pure, and yet how, in spite of all, I fell? Shall I be able to bear the angry uprising of my own burning conscience, which will bring vividly to my remembrance in that hour of terrible retribution every impure thought, every unkind word, every falsehood, every sin of which I have been guilty? Oh, this terrible Judgment to come!—How shall I meet it?—' who shall stand when He appeareth.' " (S. Matt. iii. 2).

Such may well be the the train of thought passing through your mind, dear reader, in contemplation of the awful subject I have placed before you. Believe me, it will be your own fault if yours is to be such a case as I have pictured. There is no reason why you should perish—except the reason of your own impenitence! You may be saved, if you choose! The way is open; the gates are still ajar, the arms of mercy are still outstretched! If your repentance is sincere, your confession good (1 Tim. vi. 13), your future life consistent, you cannot avoid, but you may yet safely pass through, the ordeal of

JUDGMENT TO COME.

The Parish Tracts.

FAIST AND "THE FAITH."

These two expressions are closely connected with one another, and yet they are expressive of two things which are perfectly distinct, and over each of them the battle of controversy has so long and fiercely raged that the minds of plain people have become confused, and desire to know which is which, and what is what.

Now, listen. God has given to every one a certain power of believing, and this power we call "faith." Secondly, God has revealed to His Church, through Christ Jesus and His Apostles, a certain collection of doctrines and truths, which He in His infinite wisdom proposes for man's acceptance. This body of doctrine we call "The Faith." Faith, then, is simply the power which enables a man to grasp and believe THE FAITH. And the Christian who has sufficient faith to grasp and believe the whole body of Christ's doctrine, so far as it has been revealed to him, is said to be "justified" by that faith. The one, you see, is internal in the heart, the

E

other is external in the Church. "Wherefore, that we are justified by faith only is a most wholesome doctrine, and very full of comfort," (Article XI.) to those who rightly understand the doctrine, but a very pitfall of snares to such as do not. If, then, I ask you, "Are you a believer?" I mean, has God given you, and have you realised that He has given you, such an implicit, earnest faith that you do sincerely believe, as far as you know them, all the truths which He has revealed to His Church?

There need, then, be no battle or controversy over "Faith," provided only you take care to remember that, according to Scripture, all faith is worthless unless it *influences our conduct* so that we act according to our belief, for "faith without works is dead." (S. James ii. 20.)

When, however, we come to consider our second subject, I fear we shall find too much cause for controversy, such perverted and erroneous ideas are everywhere prevalent as to what *is* "The Faith" which every Christian must believe. The importance of the subject is not disputed; the whole Bible bears witness that it is a matter of life and death to the soul to believe aright. What, then, is to become of those who go from one "place of worship" to another entirely regardless whether true doctrine or heresy is preached? S. Paul says: —"Now the Spirit speaketh expressly that in the latter times some shall depart from THE FAITH, giving

heed to seducing spirits, and doctrines of devils."
(1 Tim. iv. 1.) In 2 Cor. xiii. 5, the same Apostle
warns us :—" Examine yourselves whether ye be in
THE FAITH "—*i.e.*, not whether ye believe, but as to
what ye believe ; whether what you believe is that
" one Faith " (Eph. iv. 5), " once delivered," for
which S. Jude bids us " earnestly to contend." (S.
Jude, 3.)

Now, as to what is " The Faith " which is to be
believed, there are only two views of sufficient importance to bring before you. First, there is the view
which is held by those who have separated from
the Church, and which may be shortly stated thus :—
In order to be saved, you must believe that Jesus
Christ died to save sinners, at all events some
sinners ; and you are, if possible, to believe that you
are one of those sinners for whom Christ died. If
you do this you " believe in Jesus," and you will
undoubtedly be saved ; for Scripture says, " Believe
on the Lord Jesus Christ, and thou shalt be saved."
(Acts xvi. 31.) I think this is a fair statement of
what most of the sects teach as being " The Faith,"
as far as is necessary for man's salvation.

Secondly, there is the view taught through all
ages by the one Holy Church of God, and which
may be stated briefly thus :—In order to be saved,
you must believe in God the Father, God the Son,
and God the Holy Ghost, and in everything that
either of these Three Persons has done, or is doing

E 2

for the souls of men. Now you see at once, dear
reader, how narrow is the one view, and how broad
the other. You see how the first seizes hold of the
doctrine of the Atonement (that is, the doctrine that
Christ died for sinners), and presses that one point
almost to the exclusion of every other doctrine; and
how the other, that is the Church's view, while it
upholds that doctrine as indeed one of the corner-
stones of the Faith, yet insists equally upon all other
doctrines "which a Christian ought to know and
believe to his soul's health." The Creed called after
S. Athanasius expressly warns us that "in this
Trinity none is afore or after other, none is greater
or less than another," and further declares that "the
Godhead of the Father, of the Son, and of the
Holy Ghost is all one, the glory equal, the majesty
co-eternal;" and, finally, that the whole body of
doctrine and truth there gathered together is "the
Catholic FAITH, which, except a man believe faithfully, he cannot be saved." I must therefore exhort
you to pray earnestly for such power of believing
that you may receive the whole of the Truth as it
is in Jesus, not resting content till, by God's Grace,
you are possessed of both these priceless gifts,

FAITH, AND "THE FAITH."

The Parish Tracts.

LENT.

In considering the subject proposed for this Tract, it will be well to do so under the following heads :—

I. The object or purpose of Lenten observance.

II. The practical duties suitable to such observance.

I suppose it will not be disputed that the first or primary object we have in keeping Lent is the humble imitation, at howsoever great a distance, of Him Who, for our sakes, fasted forty days ; that as His life was in all points a pattern to be aimed at by His followers, so the Church has wisely directed that the forty days fast should be observed by all who would be perfect even as He is perfect ; and above all, that, as He Who knew no imperfection yet became " perfect through suffering," (Hebrews ii. 10), so must we strive after perfection in the way marked out for us by Him Who alone attained it. Thus, the first object of our observing Lent is to " follow the example of our Saviour Christ, and to be made like Him." The second object has reference to our own souls entirely, and may be described as *the personal humiliation of ourselves on account of*

our sins.   The sin-laden Christian finds it necessary
to occasionally "afflict his soul," not only by way of
sorrow as regards the past, but also as a spur to his
future efforts after holiness ; and the season of Lent
affords him just the opportunity which he needs.
Thus are the seasons of our dear Mother Church
exactly adapted to the spiritual needs of her children ; and the first two collects used in Lent, namely
those for Ash Wednesday and the First Sunday,
strikingly show us on what lines we are to proceed
in our efforts after self-abasement.   They are these :
—(1) Contrition of heart, leading to renewed repentance ; (2) Abstinence in food, implying general
self-denial.   In noticing these two principles, it is
important to notice the order in which they come.
If there be no contrition—that is, godly sorrow for
sin—any outward humiliation, whatever form it may
take, is worse than useless.   To "loose the bands
of wickedness" (Is. lviii. 6) must ever be the chief
motive of our self-affliction.   "Cry aloud, spare
not ; lift up thy voice like a trumpet, and *show my
people their transgression !*"   Those are the words of
Scripture which the Church orders her pastors to
sound in the ears of their flock on the first day of
Lent, and they describe with mighty power what
kind of a fast can alone be acceptable to God.   But
when you have taken this precaution, and have
humbled yourself with "a new and contrite heart,"
do not neglect the second principle laid down for us,

namely that of abstinence, or self-denial. Let your inward contrition of heart be outwardly manifested *by a distinct change in your mode of life* during the six weeks of Lent, remembering that only those who " sow in tears " can hope to " reap in joy," and that, although "no chastening for the present seemeth to be joyous, but grievous: nevertheless afterward it yieldeth the peaceable fruit of righteousness to them which are exercised thereby." (Heb. xii. 11.)

This brings me to consider the second part of our subject, viz., the practical duties by which we may best observe the holy season. I would class them in the following order :—

1. PRAYER. 2. FASTING. 3. ALMSGIVING.

A proper attention to the first of these, which is the most important of the three, will lead you to devote *more time* both to private prayer at home and to public worship in the Church you attend. As regards your private prayers, make your self-examination more frequent; if you do not understand how to do this, consult your clergyman, and he will help you. If unable to increase your prayers in number, try to increase the fervour or earnestness with which you say them. This can best be done by pausing a few seconds after each prayer, and thinking over the words you have just spoken to God. In regard to your public worship, strive to attend as many of the extra and special Lenten Services provided for you as you can, but especially make it a Lenten rule, if possible, to attend on one or other of the week days a celebration of Holy Communion over and above what you are usually accustomed to.

The matter of fasting is a difficult one about which to make a general rule. The very poor cannot fast in the literal sense of the word, nor is it expected of them; but even they can sometimes use self-denial in matters of food if they have the will to do it. My advice on this head, therefore, is that all who can possibly do so should make some marked difference in their food on the Wednesdays and Fridays throughout Lent; and that those whose poverty makes this impossible should exercise self-denial in some other way, by giving up on those days the use of something that gives them pleasure.

Lastly, as regards Almsgiving, which applies to all, it will be found in most cases a rule quite capable of fulfilment for every one to give throughout Lent double what he ordinarily gives. The extra amount may, of course, be given either in church, or in the personal relief of some neighbour in distress.

In making these suggestions for the observance of this solemn season, I am acting on the certain knowledge, acquired by experience, that if there is no RULE, there will practically be no

LENT.

The Parish Tracts.

No. XV.

REPENTANCE.

Some people may differ as to the relative importance of the several parts of repentance, but all are
agreed as to the immediate need of repentance itself.
It is this point, therefore, which I will speak of first.

Let me suppose, then, dear friend, that you are
living in open disregard of all religion; that you do
not worship God because you do not know Him;
that you do not fulfil even the ordinary duties of the
Christian life, because they would be wholly inconsistent with the life you lead in the world. Is this
your case? Then you are *separated* from God:
set apart by the leprosy of your own wilful mis-
deeds. Is it desirable that you should continue
in this state? You know it is not. You know you
cannot continue your indulgence in sinful courses for
long. An end must come. The only question,
therefore, is *when* shall you cease to live this life of
separation from God? When shall you begin to
return to Him? For I will believe that you have
sometimes a yearning for better things. You are
not really happy; sin does not, cannot *satisfy* you.

You are sometimes conscious, I am sure, of your miserable God-forsaken condition, and sometimes when you are surfeited with the husks of sin which are only fit for swine, you think of returning to God; that is to say, you think of *Repentance.* But not now! You will wait a little longer. There is some difficulty in your way at present, which, you think, will by-and-by be removed. You will wait till then. You will repent, *but not now!* Oh! how many are just in this condition! How many have, perhaps, just one darling sin which continually besets them, and so keeps them separate from God! And for this one sin, dear reader, you are going to give up—eternal life! Or, you are going to wait till a more convenient season arrives, and *then* you will repent! Now, if I have touched your case, will you kneel down to-night before you rest, and say this short prayer for yourself?

O GOD, FROM WHOM I AM NOW SEPARATED BY REASON OF MY SIN, DO THOU BY THY HOLY SPIRIT DRAW ME TO THEE AND GIVE ME THE GRACE OF TRUE REPENTANCE, FOR JESU'S SAKE. AMEN.

And now let me show you what are the several parts of a true and earnest Repentance:—1. Conviction of Sin; 2. Contrition for Sin; 3. Confession of Sin; 4. Forsaking of Sin.

I cannot enter into each of these at any length in one Tract. I can but briefly point out what is implied by the several expressions made use of, asking you, should you desire further explanation, to go to your clergyman whom God has set over you in spiritual things.

I.—CONVICTION OF SIN implies that the sinner has realised the terrible nature of his position as one exposed to the just wrath of God Who hateth iniquity, Who cannot pardon unrepented sin, and Who has attached the fearful penalty of everlasting death to all who die unreconciled to Him.

II.—CONTRITION FOR SIN implies that this conviction has led the sinner to a true, heartfelt, and godly sorrow for the mis-spent past, so that he is full of anxiety to make his peace with his offended Creator and Redeemer.

III.—CONFESSION OF SIN is the outward and formal acknowledgment before God, and, if desired, in the presence also of His minister, of all the sins which the penitent sinner can remember to have committed. Now it is plain that those sins cannot be remembered all at once. You cannot look back upon your whole life past, and by one act of memory, recall all the sins you have ever committed. Nay, nor a hundredth part of them! Therefore, *self-examination* is necessary before you can confess your sins. You must " examine yourself," both as regards faith (2 Cor. xiii. 5) and morals (1 Cor. xi. 28); that is to say, you must find out what doctrines of the Church you have disbelieved, and what commandments of the moral law you have disobeyed.

Then go and make your confession to God. If this confession be thorough and sincere, it is sufficient to make it before God alone in the secret chamber, and to pray for His pardon and forgiveness. But in the case of anyone who has fallen very often, or very grievously, the Church advises that the sinner should " open his grief " before some " discreet and learned minister of God's Word," and for this very important reason, as expressed in the same place, namely, that " he may receive the benefit of Absolution, together with ghostly counsel and advice to the quieting of his conscience."* And it must certainly be better for the sinner, who " cannot quiet his own conscience," to receive these two privileges which God has placed within his reach—namely, spiritual advice, and the declaration of pardon from one who is God's representative : " We are ambassadors for Christ." (2 Cor. v. 20.)

IV.—FORSAKING OF SIN is an expression which sufficiently explains itself. It means simply the total abandonment of those evil courses which are altogether fatal to a true and sincere

REPENTANCE.

* Exhortation in Communion Office.—Book of Common Prayer.

The Parish Tracts.

No. XVI.
EASTER COMMUNION.

This Tract will fall into the hands of three distinct classes of people, and I desire that it should carry a distinct message to each. These three classes are—

I. NON-COMMUNICANTS.

II. CARELESS COMMUNICANTS.

III. DEVOUT COMMUNICANTS.

I. I will speak first to NON-COMMUNICANTS.

I assume, dear friend, that you are not a Dissenter; you frequent Church Services, you enjoy Church worship. If you have sickness in your house, you send for the parish priest, not the Chapel preacher; if you want your child baptized you bring it to Church; and, when death lays its heavy hand upon your family, it is the clergyman's voice you would hear speaking words of comfort over the grave. I take all this for granted, because this Tract is written especially for Churchpeople. But though in all these and many other particulars you associate yourself with God's chosen people, there is one, and that a most vital point, on which you do not join with them. Notwithstanding all the instruction you have received, in your childhood, in Sunday-school; in your youth, in Confirmation or Bible classes; in your later years, in church, by sermons or otherwise; in spite of all these means of instruction, warning, and exhortation, you are still dear reader—alas! that I should have to charge you with it—but you are still a NON-COMMUNICANT! You welcome the Church's voice speaking to you from the pulpit, at the font, or by the bier, but you do not partake of the Church's FOOD at the Holy Altar! Now, I am not going to argue with you about Holy Communion. If you are determined to put off what is so plainly your duty by unreasonable excuses, all I can say is, "He that is unjust, let him be unjust still." (Rev. xxii. 11.) But I am sure I address many who are *hesitating*; they are not "determined" in their hitherto obstinate refusal of this means of grace; they are inwardly convinced, but they have not yet *quite made up their minds*. To such as these I speak now. Dear fellow-Churchman, I want you to be one with us —to enter fully into the covenant of grace—to "follow the Lamb whithersoever He goeth." Listen then to my short text and sermon.

THE TEXT.—"And note, that every parishioner shall communicate at the least three times in the year, of which Easter to be one." (Rubric—Book of Common Prayer.)

THE SERMON.—MAKE UP YOUR MIND TO DO
THIS ! The Holy Week preceding Easter is a good
time to prepare for your first Communion. The
Passion of Christ, which will be brought pro-
minently before you during those solemn days, may
well soften your heart and make you *sorry for sin* ;
and, if you are even then disturbed by the remembrance of any past sin, or by doubt or difficulties of
any kind, do not hesitate to go to your parish
clergyman, "or some other discreet and learned
minister of God's Word," and he will help you to
the attainment of that peace which your soul desires.

II. But perhaps my reader is a CARELESS COM-
MUNICANT ; one who frequents the Altar either too
seldom or too often. There are both of these.
Some are so careless of this solemn duty that they
go but a few times in the year ; others go often, but
without due preparation. I know not scarcely
which of these is the worst. In either case great
disrespect and dishonour is shown to our Blessed
Lord, Whose Presence in that Sacrament ought to be
such an attraction to the Christian, and Whose
Majesty therein, as King of Kings, ought to make
us so thoughtful and careful in our preparation to
meet Him there. The invitation to the banquet of
an earthly King would be accepted as often as given;
nor would a single guest presume to attend it without the wedding garment of *Preparation.* How
much more should we make it our rule in regard to

this banquet of the King of Kings, (1) to attend His courts with frequency, and (2) to duly prepare ourselves for so great a Feast. My message, then, to the careless Communicant is this:—LET THE EASTER FESTIVAL BE A NEW STARTING POINT FOR YOU. Make a very special preparation for this great annual Communion, and resolve that henceforth you will show due respect to your Saviour by the frequency of your attendance, and due honour to your King by the carefulness of your preparation.

III. Lastly, a word to the DEVOUT COMMUNI-CANT. It is your great privilege, dear soul, though they have "taken away your Lord" *to know where they have laid Him!* A cloud of mystery has indeed "received Him out of your sight," yet with the eagle's eye of faith you discern Him in the Sacramental Bread and Wine. He is *there*—and you know it! Be it yours this Easter, by a search-ing self-examination, by persevering, earnest prayer, and by thoughtful meditation on the wondrous con-nection between our dear Lord's Passion and the Holy Eucharist, *to attain a deeper realization of this wondrous mystery*, whereby Jesus is our Emmanuel, God with us! The Saviour's Presence in the Sacra-ment of His Love! What blessing, what grace, can you more ardently desire than to attain a deeper knowledge of this mystery, a firmer faith in this doctrine, through your

EASTER COMMUNION.

The Parish Tracts.

PRIVATE PRAYER.

Prayer is a Divinely-appointed means of communication between the Creator and the creature, between the Saviour and the sinner. Like Jacob's ladder, on which holy angels ascended and descended, prayer is a means provided by God whereby the desires of the soul may ascend to the throne of grace, and, in answer to which, the blessings of God may descend upon the soul of man. Being of Divine appointment, prayer has attached to it, like all other means of grace which God has ordained, certain conditions and certain promises. These conditions are very simple, whereas the promises are exceedingly large. The conditions of prayer being heard by God may briefly be summed up as follows:—

1. We must pray with a repentant spirit, sincerely bewailing our past sins, for " If I incline unto wickedness with mine heart, the Lord will not hear me." (Psalm lxvi. 16.)

2. We must not in prayer ask God for things which are unreasonable, or unsuitable to our station in life: " Let not that man think that he shall receive anything of the Lord." (S. James i. 7.)

F

3. We must pray in perfect confidence that God will hear our prayers, and answer them according to His good pleasure, as He knows will be best for us. " Fulfil now O Lord the desires and petitions of thy servants, *as may be most expedient for them.*" (Prayer of S. Chrysostom.)

If we firmly grasp these three simple conditions, we may be assured that our every prayer will be acceptable to God, and we may with perfect faith, trust in His one great promise—made by His Son, our Lord—" And all things whatsoever ye shall ask in prayer, believing, ye shall receive." (S. Matt. xxi. 22). Now, there are two kinds of prayer—Public, and Private. Of the former I have sufficiently spoken in a previous Tract;* it is therefore only with the latter I have to do just now, and I will try to put the whole point of this Tract into one simple question, viz. :—

Do you, my reader, say daily private prayer? By this I mean, do you make a regular habit of " meekly kneeling upon your knees " every morning before commencing your daily work, and every evening before retiring to rest, and then and there saying prayers to God? For if you do not do this, you are omitting what is one of the first and most important duties belonging to the Christian life. You are omitting to take counsel of Him Who alone can supply the needs of your soul, from Whom alone

---

* No. VII.—" Daily Service."

cometh " every good gift," (S. James i. 17), whether temporal or spiritual, and Who is willing to be your best friend both now and throughout eternity—even GOD. Now I know the difficulties which lie in your way, supposing you to be otherwise willing to use this means of grace: (1) You perhaps cannot read very well; (2) you have very little time in the morning and are very tired at night; and, worse than all, (3) you *don't know what to say!* These three difficulties are so often brought before me in conversation upon this subject that I am well acquainted with them. They are old friends, and although the first and second are more often offered to me as excuses than the third, I generally find that the most wicked of the " little foxes " that " spoil the vines " of my people's prayers is that one which " *doesn't know what to say.*"

Let me try, then, and give some plain hints to those who are willing to say daily private prayers, " if they had some prayers to say." Your daily prayer, dear friend, ought to embrace as nearly as possible *all the necessary parts of a complete Church Service,* and if you look at your Prayer Book you will notice these several parts in the daily Offices— (1) Confession of sin, with absolution; (2) Praise; (3) Prayers for particular objects; (4) Thanksgiving. Now if you will follow my guidance you may embrace all these different parts of prayer in your private devotions, without occupying more time than you can well afford to give. And the way to do this will be to take two of the above parts for your morning, and the remaining two for your evening prayers. Thus : Morning—Praise and Prayer ; Evening—Confession and Thanksgiving.

Now, take your Prayer Book and let us see whether we can find within its familiar pages suitable matter for these requirements. Your morning prayers might be composed as follows :—

I.—PRAISE. ✠ In the Name of the Father, &c. PSALM 23 or 150, or on Sundays, 43. I BELIEVE, &c. II.—PRAYER. Third Collect for Grace, in the Office of Morning Prayer. Our Father. The grace of our Lord.

For evening prayers you might use—

I.—CONFESSION. ✠ In the Name, &c. The General Confession in the Communion Service. Prayer for Pardon—see Collect for 21st Sunday after Trinity. II.—THANKSGIVING. The General Thanksgiving. Our Father. The Grace of our Lord.

These devotions that I have suggested, dear reader, are *not long*, they are, in fact, as short a little Service as one could possibly make for you. If you do not already possess other prayers which you like better, I hope you will use these, for I assure you your day has been a day misspent unless it has been consecrated to God by

PRIVATE PRAYER.

The Parish Tracts.

THE REAL PRESENCE.

I feel that the series of Tracts, of which this is one, would be incomplete unless it contained one exclusively devoted to the subject which stands at the head of this paper. I will tell you why this subject is so very important. It is because a variety of circumstances has caused it to be the *central point* of controversy amongst Churchpeople in these days; so much so, indeed, that our beloved Church is now unhappily almost rent in twain owing to the sharpness with which this much disputed doctrine divides it into two parties. This division amongst fellow-Churchmen is a most grievous matter, deeply to be deplored; but it is, unfortunately, fostered and encouraged by a persecuting society which collects large sums of money for the purpose of prosecuting, and if possible imprisoning, Clergymen who hold what are called "extreme views" on this and other kindred matters. I have said that it is this doctrine which divides Churchmen; so it is. Ostensibly the strife rages round such puerile matters as what the Clergyman should wear while Celebrating the Holy

Communion, where he should stand, how many
inches he may lift the chalice from off the Altar, and
what kind of bread he may use for the purpose of
the Sacrament.   But these are not really the questions at issue.   No Clergyman of what is called the
High Church party believes that these things are
worth fighting for *in themselves*; they are attacked
by the persecuting party, and defended by the
Clergy who use them, because they are, rightly or
wrongly, considered to cover the doctrine of the
Real Presence.

What, then, is this doctrine? and what is there
in it which makes it so very repugnant to a large
number of zealous Churchmen?   Well, the doctrine
is this: That Jesus Christ is REALLY PRESENT in
the Sacrament of His Body and Blood.   And the
reason why many earnest and well-meaning Churchmen condemn this doctrine is because *they* cannot
distinguish it from that doctrine which is condemned
in Article XVIII. under the name of Transubstantiation.   Before 1 have finished I hope you,
my reader, will both be able to believe the doctrine,
and also to distinguish it from that which is condemned by our Church.   And, to help you to these
conclusions, I will first explain at greater length what
I understand by the Real Presence, and then I will
tell you what I think is meant in our Article by
" Transubstantiation."   By the Real Presence, then,
it is meant—that, by the power of the Holy Ghost

exercised through the Priesthood in the Act of Consecration (for Deacons are not allowed to Celebrate Holy Communion), the elements of bread and wine, while retaining their outward form and appearance, *do* yet *become*, in a mysterious and spiritual sense, the VERY BODY AND BLOOD OF CHRIST, and, therefore, Christ is *really present* in this great Sacrament; His Body and Blood are, as our Catechism teaches us, " verily and indeed taken and received by the faithful in the Lord's Supper." And the present Bishop of Winchester, in his great work on the Articles, while carefully distinguishing the doctrine of our Church from the doctrine condemned in Article XXVIII., nevertheless declares, in regard to the reality of our Lord's Presence in this Sacrament, that even " Protestants of many different Communions " acknowledge that " The Body of Christ then received is the very Body that was born of the Virgin Mary, that was crucified, dead, and buried. For there is no other Body, no other Blood of Christ."*   Now I ask you to believe no more than this ; but I also earnestly beseech you to believe no less. The theory condemned in our Article is one which was held by many ignorant people at the time our Articles were made, and may be stated thus :—That the bread and wine become so completely changed by consecration that they are no

---

Bp. Harold Browne on the Articles.   Article xxviii., Sec. I. p. 680, Ed. 1868.

longer in any sense bread and wine, but altogether in a gross and carnal sense become the Body and Blood of Christ, and may, therefore, be worshipped as God. You will easily see the difference between this and the doctrine of the Real Presence as I have stated it to you, and you will have no difficulty in understanding why our Church should condemn the former as " overthrowing the nature of a Sacrament, and giving occasion to many superstitions."

To conclude then, I interpret the Church's teaching on this subject thus :—We believe that at every Celebration of Holy Communion our Lord and God is verily and indeed present ; believing in this spiritual and Sacramental Presence, we worship and adore Him there ; and the one reason why we urge your constant reception of that sacred food is just because we believe it to be really and truly His Body and Blood. The following passage from the " Protestant " historian, Macaulay, may well serve as a conclusion to this Tract, testifying as it does to the inseparable connection between the doctrine we are treating of and the Gospel of Christ :—" In the last century when a Catholic renounced his belief in the Real Presence, it was a thousand to one he renounced his belief in the Gospel too ; and, when the reaction took place, with belief in the Gospel, came back belief in

" THE REAL PRESENCE."*

* Essays, 1869.   " Von Ranke," p. 569.

The Parish Tracts.

THE GOSPEL.

I want in this Tract to give you, my dear people, a clear view, in a short compass, of what the Bible means when it speaks of " the Gospel." It is very important that you should be properly informed on this matter, because the expression is in these days misapplied to such an extent that, although there are more than one hundred and fifty different religious sects in this country, all teaching contradictory creeds, yet each sect professes to " believe the Gospel." This is, of course, impossible; for though there are four different books in the Bible called by that name, there is really only ONE GOSPEL, and that is " the glorious Gospel of Christ," (2 Cor. iv. 2), a short summary of which I am now going to give you.

God created man " in His own image," that is to say, in perfect purity and innocence. At the same time, God gave man a free will, which enabled him either to obey or disobey his Creator. Our first parents chose the latter course, and, by partaking of the forbidden fruit, lost their innocence and made God their enemy. By this one sin a great gulf was created between God and man, and every child that is born comes into the world tainted by the *original sin* of Adam, and thus is in a state of separation from God.   Now it is impossible for any one individual to bridge over this gulf; to redeem himself from this condition of bondage to Satan which is his birthright; for, even if it were conceivable that a man could live a perfectly pure and sinless life, that would not cancel or do away with the original corruption of his nature brought about by Eve's transgression.

This corruption of man's nature stands in the light of a debt due to God, and a debt of such a character that no human being could repay it.   It needed one who should be himself not only perfectly spotless in his life, but who should be conceived— and therefore born—without that stain of original sin of which I have spoken.   There was no such being in the world.   In the ordinary course of things there never could be such a one, therefore God, in His love for the human family He had created, devised a scheme by which the redemption of the sinner could be brought about.   " When the fulness of time was come God sent forth His Son made of a woman, made under the law, to redeem them that were under the law;" (Gal. iv. 4, 5)— that is to say, God Himself became Man, and in this way again united the Creator and the creature, so far, at least, that a bridge might now be swung over the great gulf which hitherto had separated them. This great mystery of God taking man's nature upon Himself is known by the name of the INCARNATION, and this doctrine is the foundation-stone on which is built the bridge I speak of. One thing yet remained to be done. This God-Man must offer His life as "a ransom for all," (1 Tim. ii. 6), and in this way become a propitiation, not only for the original sin of Adam, but also for all the actual sins of mankind. This was done. You are perfectly familiar with the story. The "Man Christ Jesus" died on Calvary, the "one Offering" for all sins, the just for the unjust; and by that atonement the bridge, of which the Incarnation was the foundation-stone, was completed, so that henceforth the sinner was enabled, by *crossing this bridge*, to become again united to God.

But observe, though the bridge is built, man is still possessed of that free will which belonged to our first parents, and though it is God's ardent wish that all men should be saved, (1 Tim. ii. 4), He will not compel any man to cross the bridge against his will. I think you will understand me now when I explain that by this bridge I mean the One Holy Catholic Church, into which all who would be saved must enter, (Acts ii. 47; S. Matt. xviii. 17), and of which the Ark of Noah is a true and perfect type. Now it is above all things necessary for you to bear in mind that God has not built several bridges, much less a hundred and fifty! There is but one.   That is to say, there is and can be but one true Church, and those who wilfully separate themselves from that Church are placing their souls in grave peril.   But, to resume ; once you are made by Holy Baptism a member of Christ's true Church, you are to continue while life lasts "in the Apostle's doctrine and fellowship, and in the breaking of bread, and in prayers." (Acts ii. 42.)   It is part of " the Gospel " that you are to be Confirmed, for that is part of the Apostle's " doctrine and fellowship " (Acts iii. 14, 17) ; that you are to be a Communicant, (S. John vi. 53), and that you are to accept implicitly those great Gospel Truths recited in the Creeds, the Resurrection and Ascension of Christ, and His session at the right hand of God the Father till He come to judge the quick and the dead.

Some people say that all they know or wish to know of " the Gospel " is contained in the words " Jesus died for me."   I hope I have shown you that the death of Jesus Christ for sinners, though a very important part, is only a very small part of the Gospel as we are bound to believe it ; and that it is as important to believe in the Incarnation, and its *extension* through the Church and the Sacraments, as it is to believe in the Atonement of Christ.   In a word I would have you believe the Gospel, the whole Gospel, and nothing but

THE GOSPEL.

The Parish Tracts.

No. XX.

HARVEST THANKSGIVING.

Annual Services are now held in nearly every parish throughout the country in connection with the ingathering of the harvest, and, although the day set apart for this observance has no official recognition in our Church's formularies, and therefore cannot be placed in the same rank with the recognised festivals of the Church, it is a notable fact that no series of Services are so heartily entered into by the people throughout the whole year as those to which I allude. The object of this present Tract is to help you, my reader, if possible, to take your part in the approaching Harvest Thanksgiving in such a way, and animated by such a spirit, as shall best promote the object which your parish clergyman has in view—namely, the promotion of God's glory, and the bringing of increased grace to your own soul. For all our worship must be overtaken with this twofold purpose, and we must take care always to put God first, and ourselves second. I am sorry to say this is not always done. If it were there would be less occasion for my Tract. Too often the chief

thought in people's minds at such times is the desire
to hear some eloquent preacher, while sometimes, I
am sorry to have to confess it, they are mostly
occupied with thoughts of the secular pleasures, the
feastings, and so forth, which so often accompany
the celebration of " Harvest Home."   If I can do
anything to counteract these evils then I shall not
have published this Tract in vain.

Now, first, I want to try and root out a rather selfish notion which I have found very prevalent in
country districts, the idea, I mean, that the Harvest
Thanksgiving is simply and solely an expression of
gratitude to God for the harvest that has been that
year gathered *in that particular parish*.   I have
actually known a parish where some of the parishioners were opposed to having their usual festival
" because," they said, " our harvest this year has
been so indifferent!"   So that if this idea were
carried out, whlie one county was thanking God for
the excellency of the crops, another would be holding a day of humiliation on account of the unusual
deficiency?   Here, then, is the first matter which
calls for remark.   I want to tell you what Harvest
Thanksgiving really means, and, when you understand that, you will be better prepared to keep it in
a proper way.   It means this, that so long as God
keeps His promise—which will be till time is no
more—that " seedtime and harvest shall not cease,"
it is the duty of each one of us to give Him thanks

ror the grain that *is* gathered, and for the garners that *are* filled. We are to regard ourselves individually simply as members of the great human family uniting, at a certain time in every year, to record our gratitude for His mercies which are year by year continued, and, while our hearts ought certainly to be specially uplifted for any local prosperity, our thoughts should extend to our brothers and sisters everywhere, whom the same God has blessed in a greater or less degree. Thus, *unselfishness* must be the keynote of our Harvest Festival.

Having thus put before you the only basis on which such festivals can rightly stand, I have now two practical suggestions to make as to the way in which we should *give God thanks*.

1. The HOLY EUCHARIST is God's own appointed way. The very word *Eucharist* means " giving of thanks," and the Church therefore, rightly and naturally, sets this Service before us as the best mode of approaching our Heavenly Father when we desire to open up our hearts to Him in gratitude for all His love. And I say that a Harvest Thanksgiving without a Eucharist would be a most inadequate expression of the feelings appropriate to the day. Remember what I said about being selfish. I know the evening is the time of day when it is *most convenient* for you to go to Church; and I know that at most Harvest Festivals the Evening Service is the most crowded. *But it ought not to be.* I say that

every parishioner, even if he be not a Communicant, ought to attend the Service of Holy Communion on Harvest Thanksgiving Day, because it is the public offering of "the Sacrifice of praise and thanksgiving," expressive of the thanks of the whole parish, as a community, for God's harvest gifts. Try, therefore, and *make it convenient* to do your duty in this respect, and, if you have been Confirmed, prepare also to be a meet partaker of those holy mysteries which are *first* offered to Almighty God, and *then* to His faithful servants in the Sacrament of the Altar.

II.   *Do not come empty-handed* to give God thanks.

If you are poor your offering will still be acceptable to Him who giveth all, however small it may be. But if your position in the world admits of it, bring such a gift to the Altar as will prove your unselfishness; and by that I mean a gift *which will cost you something* to give. David refused to "offer to the Lord of that which cost him nothing." So let it be with you. If your harvest thanksgiving is to be an expression of sincere thankfulness on your part for the seed-time and harvest which is past, see to it that whatever good object is brought before you at that time receives the full measure of support which you are really enabled to give. If you will receive these suggestions in the kindly spirit in which I have offered them, you will be doing much towards promoting the success of your approaching

HARVEST THANKSGIVING.

The Parish Tracts.

No. XXI.

SUNDAY.

"How to keep Sunday" is a question of vital and practical importance in every English home. Abroad it matters little, for, in most parts of the Continent, Sunday is, to all intents and purposes, abolished, while in Scotland the Puritan theory called Sabbatarianism is still so strong that a man has to do very much as his neighbours do ; whether he likes it or not, he must "keep the Sabbath." The English idea of Sunday observance is, I think, something midway between these two, and yet from the very fact that there is no general agreement as to what may or may not be done on Sunday, it happens that the question, "How to keep Sunday," is one which has to be considered and decided by each man for himself. It is to try and help some in their consideration of this matter that I write this Tract.

POINT I. THE CHRISTIAN SUNDAY IS NOT THE JEWISH SABBATH. I have no quarrel with those who make occasional use of the word Sabbath,

though I think it likely to be very misleading to the
young.   What is objectionable is, that those who
mostly cling to the Jewish word, cling with equal
vigour and determination to the Jewish thing ; so
that the Christian Sunday becomes with them in all
essential respects simply a "revised edition" of the
old Hebrew Sabbath.   I am quite sure that this is
not consistent with the spirit of Holy Scripture, still
less with what we know by tradition to have been
the received doctrine in the first and purest days of
Christianity.   The Jewish Sabbath is, with the rest
of the Jewish ceremonial law, wholly abolished, and,
if the Sunday retains some of the essential features
of the Sabbath, that is only another striking illustra-
tion of our Lord's assurance, "I am not come to
destroy (the law), but to fulfill."   (S. Matt. v. 17.)

POINT II.   Sunday is, as the Sabbath was, a DAY
OF REST.   This eternal principle of seventh-day rest
is consecrated for ever by the act of Creation itself,
and has therefore nothing to do with the Jewish
Sabbath, inasmuch as it was ordained by God more
than two thousand years before the Law was proclaimed.   This period of weekly rest is necessary to
man for two reasons ; first, to repair the exhaustion
caused by continual labour, and secondly, to give to
all people the opportunity, by withdrawing their
thoughts as well as their bodies from the scene of
their labour, of meditating on the greatness of the
Creator, and *the destiny of the soul.*   Hence Sunday

observance carries with it these three obligations :—

I. To cease from all unnecessary labour, and not needlessly to encourage the employment of labour by others on that day. Thus, theatre-going, to take an extreme instance, would involve the employment of an immense amount of labour, simply to gratify the taste of those who enjoy that kind of recreation. On the other hand, the opening of Public Museums would entail a very small amount of labour, would be a vast boon to the labouring classes themselves, and would be in no way inconsistent with a reverent observance of the holy day.

II. The consideration of the relations which exist between the Creator and the Creature, necessarily leads to our spending part of this day in WORSHIP, and, as the Service known among us as Holy Communion is the only Divinely-appointed act of worship in the Christian Church, it is the duty of every well-disposed Christian, to attend *that Service* every Sunday, if not prevented by some urgent cause. Other Services, such as Morning and Evening Prayer, are of course edifying, but they are not, like the Holy Eucharist, of Divine institution, and therefore not of the same importance. This duty is also distinctly Scriptural, for we read that on " the first day of the week " the Disciples " came together to break bread." (Acts xx. 17.)

3. Our thoughts being fixed on *the destiny of the soul*, to the exclusion of all thoughts of worldly

things, implies the obligation of our seeking other means of grace on this day; as spiritual instruction by the preaching of the Gospel, public prayer in God's house, and private meditation or reading at home. All these would be impossible were not Sunday a DAY OF REST.

POINT III. SUNDAY IS A FESTIVAL, NOT A FAST DAY. Instituted in weekly commemoration of the Resurrection of our Lord on Easter Day, the spirit of our observance, if it is to be in harmony with the Scripture idea, must be bright and joyful, not sad and gloomy. George Herbert, the Poet, speaks of Sunday thus:—"O Day most calm, most bright * * * Thou art a day of Mirth." And this is exactly the idea I would strive to impress on readers of this Tract. The calmness, and the brightness of Sunday, are not inconsistent with the joyousness of what is really a great Christian festival, and it is not difficult to find a middle path between the thoughtless frivolity of a Sunday in Paris, and the doleful severity of an Edinburgh " Sabbath." Amusement on Sunday I take to be perfectly legitimate, provided (1) it does not entail an undue amount of labour on the part of others, (2) it does not interfere with one's religious duties, and (3) it does not intrude on the public gaze so as to shock the feelings of the weaker brethren, or those who, from one cause or another, hold stricter views about

SUNDAY.

The Parish Tracts.

No. XXII.

ADVENT.

The solemn season of ADVENT is provided by the Church in order that the thoughts of Christian men and women may, for two or three weeks at the beginning of the Christian year, be fixed on two great events, one of which has taken place, the other being yet to come. These two events are (1) the First Coming of Christ some 1,800 years ago; (2) His Second Coming, in that day and hour which no man knoweth but the Father. This line of thought is clearly marked out for us in our Advent Collect, where the two Advents of Christ are referred to side by side; the first, in which He came to visit us with great humility; the second, when He *shall* come in His glorious majesty; and, as it is ordered that "this Collect is to be repeated *every day* with the other Collects in Advent until Christmas Eve," I think I rightly interpret the mind and intention of the Church when I say that she would have us spend these few weeks in special contemplation of these two great events. I hope I need not spend many words in asking you, my reader, to observe this holy season in the spirit in which the Church invites you. If you are a Communicant, you will find it most valuable and most precious as a time of refreshing, when your spiritual life may be deepened, and you yourself drawn nearer to God and His Christ. If you are not a Communicant, but only a " Church-goer," then just for you is this season provided, and if you will use it aright it may be the first step of the ladder leading you upwards, by that steep ascent, to a partaking of heavenly things. If you are a careless Christian, doing, perhaps, no great evil, as you flatter yourself, yet not walking warily in these dangerous days, thinking much of this present world, little of the world to come, mixing with worldly and perhaps evil companions, and so partaking of their unholiness, if this is your case, then certainly this Tract is a very special call, urging you to amend your ways, and so to employ the " talents " God has given you—I mean the opportunities He has put within your reach—that, at least, when He cometh, He may find His own with usury. If, however, you are none of these, but an open evil-liver, neglecting the Christ that bought you, spurning the grace that awaits you, leading a life which is in itself your surest condemnation, then here is for you *one more chance*, yet one more call, appealing to your hitherto hardened heart, wrestling with your childish, wayward spirit, imploring you to examine the ground on which you stand, and inviting you to consider most seriously whether *you are satisfied with the security* on which you have staked your immortal soul!

Now Christ came, the first time, in the most humiliating form possible, as " the carpenter's son;" when He comes again He will come in all the power and glory of the King of Kings and Lord of Lords. And each of these carries its special lesson applicable to the season we are talking of.

I. CHRIST'S FIRST COMING. He came in humility. The day of His coming is known to us as Christmas Day. This day has ever been and is still regarded as one of the greatest, and always the most generally-observed, festival in the year. Every one keeps Christmas. Why? Because it is the anniversary of Christs' first coming. Then surely it is a *religious* feast. Surely it means something more than plum pudding and mince pies! And if so, then we who are Christ's—we, who in any sense acknowledge Him—are bound to make every due preparation to welcome Him on Christmas Day. Yes; this is exactly our duty. Christ offers to make a special Advent to your soul on Christmas Day. Prepare for that coming. If you are already a Communicant, prepare and pray for some special blessing. If you are not, oh! neglect this great salvation no longer; say to yourself, by

God's grace and by the energy of my own preparation, I will receive Christ sacramentally on Christmas Day, and so shall I fitly commemorate His First Coming.

II. HIS SECOND COMING. He shall come in majesty, in great power and glory; every eye shall see Him—yes, my eye shall meet His in that day. Shall I be able to gaze on His glorious face? In other words, will I be amongst those "pure in heart" who, on that great and terrible day, shall be able to "see God?" Well, let me answer this by glancing at my present condition. Am I *now* "pure in heart," and, therefore, pure in *life!* Is my life pure? Am I a Christian in very truth, and not only in name? No! Then surely here is work for me to do this Advent season. I will turn aside from my wickedness. I will go to my Father and will say unto Him, "Father, I have sinned against Heaven and before Thee"—you know the rest! Oh, may you, dear fellow-sinner, so make ready with me to celebrate Christ's Coming on this approaching Christmas Day, that we may be prepared to meet Him when He comes again in His last and, for the unprepared sinner, most terrible

ADVENT.

The Parish Tracts.

No. XXIII.

DEATH.

You may wonder why I should write a Tract on Death. I certainly do not profess to know more about the Great Destroyer than most of my readers do, nor can I undertake to say anything new about a subject which is almost as old as sin itself. Perhaps, however, this Tract may find its way into the hands of some to whom Death has become *so* common a subject as to have lost its terrors, while it may reach the notice of others who are victims of a morbid dread of death which is inconsistent with the Christian profession.

My reader, amidst all the confusing uncertainties of this mortal life one thing is sure—you must die! Unless, indeed, you shall be among those of whom S. Paul says " We shall not all sleep," you must expect to follow those who have gone before you, and who now lie down in the long, dark night, the dark night of death. Now, to those who are prepared for this event, death has no abiding terrors. For them it is simply the voyage from earth to Paradise; from the company of worldly men and

women to that of the saints at rest; from all the
sorrows, cares, and anxieties of life in the world, to a
peaceful resting in Abraham's bosom, in joyful ex-
pectation of the summons to enter into the everlasting joy of their Lord. But for those who are *not
prepared*, oh! how different must be the first warning
of approaching death! Let the reader of this Tract
calmly weigh in his mind what his feeling would be
if he were informed that this very day God would
require his soul. And it is no impossible surmise.
Death has come to many a one with less warning
than that. Millions of souls now awaiting the dread
rising to damnation would tell you, if they could, that
they would give all they ever possessed for a few
hours in which to reconsider their past conduct, for
a short interview with the very Clergyman whose
continued warnings they despised on earth, for even
a few moments in which to cry to God for mercy,
for pardon, for repentance. Yes! go and ask the
souls, the myriads of lost souls, now anticipating the
dread sentence of their final doom—ask them, I say,
" What think ye of death?" and they will tell you
it is a thing most terrible, an event of the most
appalling significance, a crisis for which, if they had
but another chance, they would make a life-long
preparation. And yet, though what I am saying is
nothing new, though all this and much more is
already known amongst men, go where I will I find
the utmost unconcern everywhere prevailing on the

part of living men and women as to that fierce
enemy which dogs their path night and day, which
stands across their threshold each time they enter or
leave the house, which hovers over their slumbers
like a dark thunder-cloud each night, and which
awaits them sooner or later with a certainty which
they cannot gainsay! Everywhere is death known
to be the last great enemy, everywhere, on all sides
and constantly are its terrors seen by the bedside of
unconverted sinners; yet those very persons who see
most of death are often the very ones who give the
least heed to its approach in their own case—so true
is it, even in sacred things, that

"*Familiarity breeds contempt.*"

Now the whole lesson of death is perfectly set
forth in words of inspiration to which I would invite
the earnest attention of every devout reader; I refer
to that part of the fifteenth chapter of First Corin-
thians which is read as the lesson in the Burial
Office. If that sublime and magnificent passage of
Holy Scripture were only translated into words
which all could understand, I would urge its being
printed as a Divine Tract and distributed broadcast
throughout the land, but there are expressions in it
which are too difficult to permit of this. Still let all
who will, go and drink deeply of that fountain of
living water. Go and learn there the two great
lessons of death, which I will briefly set forth in
conclusion as follows :—

I. To the Penitent. Death is the bridge across which you must pass before you can reach the promised land. The toll of mortality must be paid, for " corruption cannot inherit incorruption ;" yet, when this is achieved, then death, in your case, is " swallowed up in victory," and as in Adam all die, so in Christ shall you be made alive, alive for ever in the resurrection of the just, alive unto God through Jesus Christ our Lord !

II. To the Impenitent. Death is to be for you, unpardoned sinner, the crowning misfortune of your miserable life ! If you *will* harden your heart you cannot enter into His rest. If you will despise the proffered mercies of God, the love of Christ which passeth knowledge, the warning voice of His Blessed Spirit, then die you must, only to die a second and yet more miserable death " where their worm dieth not." Therefore, take this warning now given you; AWAKE TO RIGHTEOUSNESS AND SIN NOT ! for it is spoken to your shame that you have not the knowledge of God, (1 Cor. xv. 34). If you will turn now there is yet time, and you may even yet secure for yourself a peaceful and a happy

DEATH.

The Parish Tracts.

No. XXIV.

HEAVEN OR HELL.

The question of all questions, my friend! For you, for me, for all, this *must* be the one great undying question, which should excite our keenest anxiety, and cause our heart-strings to vibrate with intensest solicitude. Life and Death are both great mysteries, full of difficulty, incapable of explanation, defying analysis, *yet experienced by all.* We all live, and know something of what life is. We all die, and therefore, by the ever-occurring death of those around us, have an experimental knowledge to a certain extent of what death is. The *fact* of life is impressed upon us by every movement of our body, the *certainty* of death is brought home to us by the experience and testimony of a thousand generations. But after life is over, after death has occurred, what then, my friend? Here you have no experience to fall back upon.

If some few out of the millions of created beings have been brought back from death to life, they have not furnished us with any account of their experience in the other world.   The little lad whom Elijah raised from the dead has left us no record; the only son of the widow of Nain is silent; Lazarus has nothing to tell us of those four days during which his soul was separated from his body.   No! in regard to the awful question of "Heaven or Hell," I repeat, you have no human experience to guide you in making up your mind. You must depend for all your information on the Truth as it is revealed in the written Word of God.   That Word tells you that that there is a Heaven, there is a Hell.   It declares most positively that one or other of these places is the goal to which every immortal soul is journeying, and that, inasmuch as the eternal destination of the soul is *fixed at death*, now during your life-time, now while you are in health, now while you have yet time, *now* is the season for you to calmly ponder and once and for ever decide for yourself whether you will GO TO HEAVEN, or whether you will GO TO HELL! These are startling words. I mean them to be so. Remember, they are only startling because they are true.

Now, the Bible, mark you, does not profess to give you a literally exact and accurate description of either Heaven or Hell, but, oh! surely, dear reader, it tells you enough to make you long for the one and dread the other.   Let us see first, then—

I. WHAT IS HEAVEN?   It is the *Home of God*, therefore it must be full of joy, peace, and love.

The jewelled foundations, the gates of pearl, the crystal stream, the many crowns, the golden censers, the pure white linen, the golden girdles, the harpers harping with their harps, all these and sundry other such like expressions are found in the Book of Revelations as descriptive of Heaven. But no one surely imagines them to be anything more than an attempt to convey to human minds some idea of the scene around the Throne of God. I maintain at least that the most glowing descriptions in the Bible fall infinitely short of what Heaven will be to those blessed ones who shall find their home there. No human language is adequate to picture to our mind either the nature or the extent of the joys of Heaven. Enough for us to know that God shall wipe away all tears from our eyes there, that there shall be no more sorrow nor crying, neither shall there be any more pain, for the former things are passed away, and, behold I make all things new. (Rev. xxi. 4, 5.) Now, in contrast to this I ask—

II. WHAT IS HELL? Some people do not believe in a real Hell : a very convenient creed for the workers of iniquity. They say (what is quite true—there is always a *little bit* of truth in every denial of true doctrine) they say that *the Bible language about Hell* is also to a large extent figurative, and, therefore, conveys no accurate idea of what Hell is. I quite grant this. The language used *is* but figurative, and the worm that dieth not, the fire unquenchable, the endless smoke from the bottomless pit, the brimstone and the dragon, these, I grant you, are but figurative expressions, used in order to convey to our human intellect some idea of what the pains of Hell will be. But it is as true in this case, as in the case above, that the language used does not express one-millionth part of what the pains and agonies of Hell will really be. Language is utterly inadequate to this task, and just as Heaven will be infinitely more glorious than the mind of man can conceive, so will Hell be over and over again more terrible than the Bible has described it to us. And of Hell this at least is true, that there shall be weeping and gnashing of teeth for ever, that the inhabitants thereof shall "gnaw their tongues for pain," and that in that dreadful abode the company will not only include devils and angels, but the "fearful, and unbelieving, and the abominable, and murderers, whoremongers, and sorcerers, and idolaters, and all liars shall have their part" in that second death. Oh! surely here is enough for you to know, my brother, or my sister. Surely you will at once wrestle with this great and most momentous question. Ask yourself again and again, day by day, which is it to be for me—oh! my God, which shall be my portion for ever,

HEAVEN OR HELL?

OPINIONS OF THE PRESS.

————:o:————

"These are the outcome of an original and excellent idea which the Rev. J. H. Buchanan has put into form for the purpose of conveying Church doctrines into the minds of his people. * *. * The idea is to localise these Tracts as magazines are localised. * * * We can recommend the Clergy to adopt the plan. * * * '—*Church Times.*

"We desire to say a word of hearty commendation on behalf of the PARISH TRACTS, by Rev. J. H. Buchanan. They are thoroughly sound, and just the thing for distribution among the uninstructed or careless. * * *"—*Church Review.*

"In the PARISH TRACTS * * * we seem to recognise an unusually strong and telling faculty of putting religious truths into clear and definite forms, and into such language as the poor and uninstructed will understand and be impressed by."—*Literary Churchman.*

"A series of **very** short and effective Tracts, explaining the principal doctrines and usages of the Church. We strongly recommend them."—*Churchman's Companion.*

"We have carefully read each of the published numbers, and could hardly say which is the best. Nothing could excel them for distribution, either among the artisans of our crowded busy towns, or the agricultural labourers in country parishes."—*Hull Church Gazette.*

"The Rev. J. H. Buchanan deserves the thanks of Churchmen for his admirable series of Tracts. * * * There is an arresting power in the writer's style which accounts for the success which has so justly attended the issue of his series."—*Church Review.*

www.ingramcontent.com/pod-product-compliance
Lightning Source LLC
LaVergne TN
LVHW061219060426
835508LV00014B/1366